Shellfish COOKERY
Delicacies from the West Coast

Ann Kask

Ptarmigan Press
Campbell River, British Columbia

Copyright © 2004 Ann Kask

All Rights Reserved

First Printing December 2004   Fourth Printing September 2007
Second Printing February 2007   Fifth Printing May 2008
Third Printing May 2007

Library and Archives Canada Cataloguing in Publication

Kask, Ann
    Shellfish cookery : delicacies from the West Coast/ Ann Kask

Includes Index.
ISBN 0-919537-66-9

1. Cookery (Shellfish) I. Title.
TX753.K37 2004   641.6'94   C2004-906562-9

Front cover photography by Gordon Kirk
Mussel pottery by Jan and Mike Sell, Mussels & More Pottery Inc.
Composition and Design by Kask Graphics Ltd., Campbell River, BC
www.kaskgraphics.com

Published by Ptarmigan Press
1372 - 16th Avenue
Campbell River, BC V9W 2E1 Canada
www.ptarmiganpress.com

Printed and bound in Canada on acid free paper

This cookbook was produced as a fundraiser for the Team Diabetes Canada program. The recipes do not necessarily represent those recommended by the Canadian Diabetes Association. For more information, please consult your doctor, the Diabetes Education Centre in your area, a registered dietitian or the Canadian Diabetes Association web site - www.diabetes.ca

Foreword

I am pleased to be asked to write the forward to Shellfish Cookery, the second of Ann Kask's cookbooks that support the Canadian Diabetes Association, Team Diabetes Canada.

I am delighted that an entire cookbook has been devoted to shellfish. For many years shellfish were thought to be high in cholesterol and were discouraged, especially for those individuals at risk for heart disease. We know now that this is an unnecessary restriction. In fact, most shellfish are low in saturated fat, a source of omega-3 fatty acids and high in many essential nutrients. As a registered dietitian, I now encourage people to include shellfish dishes in their diets.

The local chefs, restaurateurs and shellfish growers who contributed to this cookbook deserve recognition. Campbell River, a coastal community, has long been known for its salmon, but restaurants that serve fresh, local seafood of all kinds are wise to take advantage of these other wonderful resources available to them. The subtitle of this book says it all - "Delicacies from the West Coast".

I continue to be impressed with Ann's efforts to raise money for diabetes. The predictions for increases in the incidence of diabetes in Canada are alarming. Money that will be put towards research into its causes, treatments, management and education is desperately needed, and diabetes educators appreciate fundraising efforts that support such research. This project is an excellent example of how one person can make a huge difference and benefit all Canadians. Thank you Ann.

Claire Lightfoot, RD, MEd, CDE
Registered Dietitian, Certified Diabetes Educator
Campbell River, BC
November, 2004

Acknowledgements

Books such as this come together only through the efforts of many people. I am honoured that so many of the people that contributed to *Salmon Cookery* joined me again to create *Shellfish Cookery*.

Thank you to all the chefs, restaurateurs, shellfish growers and people who donated recipes and instructions. These form the backbone of the book.

Thank you Debbie LeMay for your tireless collection and followup to make sure that all the recipes actually made it into the book, and to both you and your husband Gordon LeMay for proofing recipes.

Thank you Bertha Seabolt for your encouragement and recipe collection.

Thank you Claire Lightfoot for writing the foreward to the book.

Thank you Gordon Kirk for your photography on the front cover.

Thank you Kathy Morrison for providing the first recipe, to get me inspired and to Dennis Vaughan and Dwight Walden, who suggested that I should do a followup to *Salmon Cookery*.

Thank you Susan Carlson of the Canadian Diabetes Association, Nanaimo for your encouragement and also for getting some Nanaimo shellfish recipes.

Thank you Brent Petkau for your conversations about oysters.

Thank you Dave Battison for helping me prepare for the Honolulu marathon while putting this cookbook together.

Thank you Shannon Kask ("prawns are O.K.") for designing the covers and creating a book out of many loose pages.

And finally, thank you to my husband, Lorne for spending hours helping me proof recipes and for continued support of my involvement with Team Diabetes Canada, and to Alex Kask for carefully checking spelling.

Table of Contents

Forward 3

Acknowledgements 4

Introduction 6

Shellfish Tips
      Oysters 8
      Clams 10
      Mussels 11
      Crabs 12
      Prawns and Shrimp...13
      Scallops...14

Appetizers 15

Soups, Salads, Etc.
      Soups, Stews..54
      Salads..68
      Wraps and more...70

Entrées
      Prawns, Shrimp 80
      Crab...95
      Oysters 96
      Mussels 101
      Clams 108
      Seafood 110
      Scallops...112
      Lobster..118

Dessert 120

Index..123

Introduction

Shellfish Cookery: Delicacies from the West Coast has been produced in support of the Canadian Diabetes Association's Team Diabetes Canada initiative.

TEAM DIABETES CANADA recruits participants for marathons, adventure races, 24-hour mountain bike relays and the Canadian Ironman Triathlon. Since the program's launch in 2000, more than 1000 people from across Canada have raised over $4.2 million for diabetes research, education, service and advocacy. Team Diabetes Canada members set an example of a healthy active lifestyle which is important in the prevention and management of diabetes.

DIABETES is a chronic disease that has no cure. It is characterized by the body's inability to produce or properly use insulin. Insulin is a hormone that is needed to convert sugar, starches and other food into the energy needed for daily life.

Over 2 million Canadians have diabetes. Ten percent have Type 1 diabetes which is caused by the body's failure to produce insulin. This form of diabetes is generally diagnosed in childhood or early adulthood.

The other ninety percent have Type 2 diabetes which results when the body fails to make enough insulin or properly use insulin. Type 2 diabetes is most commonly found in Canadians over the age of 45 and is linked to heredity and lifestyle factors such as obesity and inactivity.

Diabetes is one of the leading causes of death by disease in Canada, and it is estimated that at least $9 billion is spent annually on it's treatment and related diseases. Heart disease, stroke, kidney failure, adult blindness and amputation are some of the serious health problems associated with this disease.

Shellfish

TIPS

Shellfish Tips

There is nothing like fresh shellfish, gathered and cooked fresh from the sea, On the West Coast we are fortunate to have many kinds of shellfish that can be collected recreationally, if you are fortunate enough to be able to get out to the right location and have the proper equipment. Clams, crabs, mussels, oysters, scallops, shrimp and prawns are all found in the waters of the Pacific.

Before gathering any shellfish, be sure to check for any closures in the area. Contact Fisheries and Oceans Canada at www.pac.dfo-mpo.gc.ca or the 24 hour Shellfish Information line at 604-666-2828.

Most often one has to buy shellfish. **Always buy your seafood from a reputable source.**The following are some guidelines for selecting, storing and preparing shellfish.

Oysters

There has long been the warning about eating oysters only during months with an "R" in the name. This is a myth. Oysters are edible all year round. They are best raw during the winter months because they spawn in the summer months and as a result may be softer and more fatty at this time of year.

Selecting oysters
Live oysters should have tightly closed shells, or they should close readily after being tapped. A gaping shell indicates that the oyster is dead and no longer edible. Avoid oysters with broken or damaged shells.

Fresh shucked oyster meats should be plump and firm and have a fresh, mild saltwater scent. They should be discarded if they smell sulphurous or feel slimy. The oyster meats should be packed in their own juices (liquor), which should be clear.

Storing oysters

Live oysters should be stored in the refrigerator cupside down, covered with a damp towel. Oysters need to breathe and will not survive in airtight bags or containers or in water. Stored in the refrigerator at a temperature below 40° F (5° C) or ideally 34 ° F (1° C) , oysters can be kept alive for at least 10 days.

For freshly shucked oysters, strain the liquor through a double layer of cheesecloth. Oysters and strained liquor may be stored in a tightly covered container in the refrigerator for up to 10 days.

To freeze oysters, wash oysters in brine (1 Tbsp/15 mL salt for each quart/litre of water). Drain and pack in freezer containers, covering with strained oyster liquor. Put lid on securely and keep frozen below 0° F (-18° C) for up to 3 months.

To thaw oysters, let stand in refrigerator overnight or place sealed container in a bath of cold water for a few hours. Do not thaw oysters at room temperature. Do not refreeze thawed oysters.

How to shuck an oyster (Marcel Creurer)

Before shucking the oysters, scrub the shells with a brush under cold running water. Do not let the oysters stand in the water.

• Place the oyster on a hard surface, flat shell up.
• Insert a shucking knife between the shells at the three o' clock position. Wear a pair of sturdy gloves to protect against possible nicks and cuts. If you find it hard to insert the knife, first chip a portion of the "bill" creating a small opening.
• Cut the large abductor muscle where it attaches to the top shell; pry the shell off by twisting the oyster knife.
• If the oyster is to be served on the half shell, leave it in place in the deep bottom shell. Otherwise, cut the abductor muscle along the deep shell and slip the oyster meat from the shell into a container, along with the nectar.

You may also place the whole oyster in a pot of boiling water only long enough for the shell to partially open, thus allowing the knife to be more easily inserted. Or, try quick freezing the oyster in order to more easily open.

Oysters may also be partially opened in the microwave. Cook three or four oysters at a time for 1 minute.

Oyster presentation tips (Brent Petkau)
Give each oyster the "sniff" test while shucking to make sure it is fresh smelling.

When laying out the oysters for serving, use rock salt or pebbles to keep them level on the platter. This will also help retain the liquor in the shell. For an elegant presentation, use the top shell as a "saucer" for the bottom shell - no wasted shells.

Clams

Selecting clams
Fresh clams should have tightly shut shells. Avoid shells that are chipped, broken or damaged. A gaping shell which does not close when tapped sharply indicates that the clam is dead and should be discarded.

Shucked clams should have plump meat with clear liquid.

Storing clams
Live clams can be kept alive in a refrigerator for up to 7 days when kept at 34° F (1° C) and sprayed regularly with fresh seawater. Ensure that live clams can breathe by storing them in an open box or sack.

Shucked clams can be stored in a tightly covered container with strained liquor in the refrigerator below 40° F (5° C) no longer than 2 days.

Shucked clams may be frozen for up to 4 months packed in a freezer container, covered with strained liquor. Put lid on securely and keep below 0° F (-18° C).

To thaw clams, let stand overnight in the refrigerator or place sealed container in a bath of cold water for a few hours. Do not thaw at room temperature. Do not refreeze shucked clams.

Purging clams
Live clams should be purged before eaten. This is to allow them to cleam themselves of ingested sand. One method is to sprinkle oatmeal over a bucket of clams stored in salt water. The clams will ingest the oatmeal and spit out the sand.

If you have the time and the opportunity, you can hang clams in salt water off a dock or a boat for a few days to purge them.

Mussels

Selecting mussels

Live mussels should have tightly closed shells or shells that snap shut when tapped. The shells should remain closed after being gently squeezed. Discard mussels that have gaping or broken shells, or do not open when fully cooked. Watch for heavy shells that may be full of sand and shells that feel light and loose when shaken; the mussels are likely dead.

Shucked mussels should have plump meat with clear liquid.

Storing mussels

Mussels can be kept alive in a refrigerator for up to 3 to 4 days when stored dry below 50° F (10° C). Store them in a single layer covered with a damp cloth. Do not put them in a plastic bag or immerse them in fresh water, as they need to breathe.

Shucked mussels may be stored in a tightly covered container with strained liquor in the refrigerator below 40° F (5° C) for 1 or 2 days.

Shucked mussels may be frozen for up to 4 months packed in a freezer container, covered with strained liquor. Put lid on securely and keep below 0° F (-18° C).

To thaw mussels, let stand in refrigerator overnight or place sealed container in a bath of cold water for a few hours. Do not thaw at room temperature. Do not refreeze thawed mussels.

Debearding mussels

The beard (byssus) is the thick fibres at the narrow end of the mussel. Remove the beard by pulling from the top to the bottom. Another option is to trim the beard off with a sharp knife or scissors.

Crabs

Selecting crabs
Live crabs should be active and have hard shells (unless a soft-shelled variety). Look for crabs that are heavy for their size (more meat).

Cooked whole crabs should have hard shells and a slightly sweet fresh smell. Cooked crab meat should be white with red or brown tints. Avoid crab meat with a fishy odour or dried out meat.

Storing crabs
Live whole crabs can be covered with a damp cloth and stored in a refrigerator below 40° F (50° C) for up to 12 hours.

Whole cooked crab can be refrigerated but should be used within 24 hours. Fresh crab meat should be stored below 34° F (1° C) and used within 3 days.

Whole cooked crab may be frozen for up to 2 months. Place in a plastic freezer bag, exclude air, seal tightly and keep below 0° F (-18° C).

Cooked crab meat should be packed into freezer containers and covered with a fresh brine (2 tsp/10 mL salt for 1 cup/250 mL water). Allow 1/2 inch headspace, place lids on securely and keep below 0° F (-18° C) for up to 2 months.

Cleaning crabs (Crabby Bob's way)
Place the crab on its back and hit it in the centre with a wedge or knife. Next, grab all the legs and roll them inward and pull them outward. Give each side a snapping shake to remove the innards. Finally, remove gills that are attached to the legs.

Cooking crabs (Crabby Bob's way)
After bringing the water to a boil, add some pickling salt (non-iodized) - one handful per 4 to 5 crabs is plenty. Add crab and wait until water comes back to a boil. Ten minutes in boiling water will cook crab thoroughly. Cool the legs with cold water and enjoy your crab feast!

How to crack a crab
Separate legs from each other, one at a time, leaving the portion with the body meat attached. Crack the shell of each body section and the claw using a nutcracker or pliers. Meat can then be removed using the tip of the leg or a small pick or fork.

Prawns and Shrimp

Selecting prawns and shrimp
Live prawns and shrimp should be active. Fresh unshelled prawns or shrimp should have shiny firm shells that are tightly attached to their bodies. Shelled prawns or shrimp should have a firm texture and be moist and translucent. Avoid prawns or shrimp that smell of ammonia.

Cooked prawns or shrimp should have firm bodies that retain a curled shape. Avoid prawns or shrimp that are flat or limp.

Storing prawns and shrimp
Store uncooked or cooked prawns and shrimp in a refrigerator below 40° F (5° C) for up to 3 days.

Prawns or shrimp may be frozen for up to 3 months. Shell, remove sand vein and wash in brine (1 Tbsp/15 mL salt to 1 quart/litre of water) and drain uncooked shrimp. Package in freezer bags, exclude air, seal tightly and keep frozen below 0° F (-18° C).

How to peel and devein prawns and shrimp
To peel the prawns or shrimp easily, take a sharp knife or scissors and cut down the middle of the back shell from head to tail. Break open the shell and pull it off leaving the tail attached, if desired. Pull or wash out the vein under cold running water and rinse.

How to butterfly prawns and shrimp
With a sharp knife, cut almost all the way through along the back of the prawn or shrimp. Spread both halves open.

Scallops

Selecting scallops
Live scallops should have tightly closed shells, or if open, they should shut when tapped. They should have a clean scent. Avoid scallops with gaping shells or shells that are cracked or chipped.

Fresh shucked scallop meat should be moist looking, firm and have a sweet and briney odour. Usually only the round abductor muscle is sold.

Storing scallops
Live scallops may be stored covered with a damp cloth in a refrigerator below 50° F (10° C) for 2 to 3 days. Scallops need to breathe. Do not put them in a plastic bag. Avoid contact with fresh water, which will kill them.

Shucked scallops may be stored in a tightly covered container in the refrigerator below 40° F (5° C) for 1 or 2 days.

Shucked scallops may be frozen for up to 3 months. Wash in brine (1 Tbsp/15 mL to 1 quart/litre) of water. Drain and package in plastic freezer bags. Exclude air, seal tightly and keep below 0° F (-18° C).

To thaw scallops, let stand in refrigerator overnight or place sealed container in a bath of cold water for a few hours. Do not thaw at room temperature. Do not refreeze thawed scallops.

Shucking scallops
Scallops may be shucked like oysters (see how to shuck an oyster page 9), or may be opened by putting them in a hot oven.

Appetizers

Crabby Bob's Famous and Favourite Crab Dip

Warning: This dip is addictive!

2	cooked crabs	2
8 oz	package cream cheese	250 g
1 Tbsp	Worcestershire sauce	15 mL
1 Tbsp	lemon juice	15 mL
1/4 cup	finely chopped onion	60 mL
1/2 cup	chili sauce	125 mL

Mix cream cheese, Worcestershire sauce, lemon juice and onion well. Spread on serving platter.

Spread chili sauce on top of bottom layer.

Top with shredded crab meat from the two cooked crabs.

Serve with crackers (Triscuits are best for this dip).

Enjoy.

Now you must face the same dilemma as Crabby Bob faces on a daily basis - are you being invited to functions for your awesome personality or your equally awesome crab dip???

Bob Hutter
Crabby Bob's Seafood

Extreme King Crab

Experience what only Kings and Queens did from yesteryears.

1 lb	*King crab legs, cut into 1 inch (2.5 cm) lengths	500 g
1 cup	water	250 mL
1 tsp	salt	5 mL
1 1/2 Tbs	white wine	25 mL
1 tsp	lemon juice	5 mL
2 Tbsp	garlic, fine mince	30 g
1/2 cup	butter	125 g
1 cup	Champagne	250 mL

Place crab aside and place water, salt, white wine and lemon juice in a pot. Bring to a boil. Place crab in pot and cover. Cook only to reheat the crab, as most King crab is previously cooked.

Melt butter and reduce on low heat until all milk whey is reduced to zero. Quickly add garlic and remove from heat. Place in heated dish.

With a cocktail fork, remove the crab from its shell and immerse in Champagne for 5 seconds. Remove from Champagne and immerse in hot garlic butter for about 3 seconds. Place in mouth. Let your taste buds explode.

*Dungeness crab may be substituted for the King crab.

Dennis Vaughan
Royal Coachman Pub and Catering

Hot Crab Dip

This is an all-time favourite. I use fresh crab meat, but frozen or canned works well too. This appetizer can be made the night before serving and it also freezes well.

6 oz	crab meat	170 g
12 oz	cream cheese	340 g
1 1/2 Tbs	milk or white wine	23 mL
1 Tbsp	finely chopped green onions	15 mL
1/8 tsp	Dijon Mustard	.5 mL

Blend cream cheese with milk or wine until soft and smooth.

Add crab meat, onion and mustard and blend well.

Place mixture in an oven-to-table dish. Refrigerate overnight or proceed to bake immediately.

Bake in a 350° F (180° C) for 20 to 25 minutes or until hot and bubbly.

Serve with nacho chips or crackers such as Vegetable Thins.

Ann Kask

Stuffed Crab Claws

12	crab claws	12
1 lb	shelled shrimp or prawns	500 g
1	egg white	1
1/4 cup	cornstarch	60 mL
2 cups	breadcrumbs	500 mL
2/3 tsp	salt	3 mL
pinch	sesame oil	pinch
pinch	ground white pepper	pinch

Steam crab claws until cooked. Remove shell (except one pincer of each claw).

Wash shrimp or prawn meat. Wipe dry and mash.

Add salt, sesame oil and white pepper. Stir vigorously until sticky and toss it 7 or 8 times. Stir well to form shrimp mash.

Divide into 12 portions.

Dust cornstarch on crab claws. Moisten hand with egg white.

Stuff shrimp mash on crab claw.

Coat with mixture of cornstarch and breadcrumbs.

Deep fry over medium heat (140° F/330° C) until golden brown.

Serve with your own presentation.

Joseph Au
Best Wok

Glazed Oysters

A Cortes Island Oysterfest favourite.

	enough medium-size fresh oysters, shucked and drained to produce	
1 quart	oyster meat	1 L
1/2 tsp	butter	2 mL
1 Tbsp	lime marmalade	15 mL
1 Tbsp	stone ground mustard	15 mL

Steam open medium-size oysters; shuck and discard the shells.

Refrigerate and let drain overnight.

In a large, heavy frying pan, melt butter, lime marmalade and mustard. Heat until it starts to turn brown.

Add drained oyster meat. Cook 1 to 2 minutes until they glaze.

Serve hot.

An interesting variation is to add 1 teaspoon (2 mL) curry powder to the glaze.

Marcel Creurer
Silent Harvest Inc.

Barbequed Oysters with Devil's Butter

**fresh oysters, allow at least 6 oysters
per person**

Devil's Butter

1 cup	salted butter	250 mL
1 cup	chopped fresh parsley	250 mL
2 Tbsp	strong grainy Dijon mustard	30 mL
4-6 Tbsp	Louisiana Hot Sauce	60 - 90 mL
1 Tbsp	lemon juice from fresh lemons	15 mL
	salt, to taste	

Combine ingredients in a saucepan and bring to a slow boil. Reduce heat and simmer for approximately 1 hour. Stir sauce vigorously before applying to oysters.

*Place oysters that have been scrubbed on the barbeque, medium heat. Wait until they start to open, then pry open the top of the oyster. Do this carefully so as not to spill the nectar in the oyster.

Once top is off oyster, put a teaspoon (5 mL) of Devil's Butter on each oyster and cook at high heat, adding more Devil's Butter as needed.

*When placing oysters on the barbeque, I try to have some small pebbles handy to place under the oysters that won't sit level. This keeps the natural juices in the shell.

Also, my preference when barbequing oysters is to shuck the oysters before placing them on the barbeque, being careful not to spill the nectar (natural juices), and cooking until partially cooked, then adding the Devil's Butter. Either way will work, but I find if I'm cooking for a larger group, my way seems more efficient.

**Fred Picard
Picard's Bed and Breakfast**

Cortes Island Barbequed Oyster Variations

Barbequed oysters can be eaten straight or with a squeeze of lemon. If you wish to get more elaborate than that, here are a few ideas.

Spinach and Feta Cheese Stuffing

Stuff a small amount of **spinach** and/or **Feta cheese** into the shell and allow cheese to melt over the oyster.

Brent Petkau, Oysterman

Asian Delight

7/8 cup	sesame oil	200 mL
7/8 cup	Tamari sauce	200 mL
1	medium ginger root, finely chopped	1
2	heads of garlic (lots of garlic)	2

Combine the ingredients in a saucepan and bring to a slow boil. Reduce heat and simmer for approximately 1 hour. Remember to stir sauce vigorously before applying to oysters.

For 5 dozen oysters.

Pesto and Feta Cheese Topping

2	packages Pesto (Olivieri brand)	2
14 oz	Feta cheese	400 g

Slice cheese into small cubes. Apply a teaspoon (5 mL) of pesto to each oyster and top with a cube of Feta cheese while cooking.

Fred Picard
Picard's Bed and Breakfast

Oysters with Mustard

medium-size oysters
mayonnaise
French mustard

Remove top shell from medium-size oyster. Top with a mixture of 2/3 mayonnaise and 1/3 French mustard.

Cook in the barbeque until golden.

Ostras Gratinadas (Brazil)

small-size oysters
mild cheese (German butter cheese
works well)
mozarella cheese, grated
sliver of hot chili pepper
small fresh parsley leaf

Steam open small-size oysters; remove and discard top shell.

Cover each oyster with a mild cheese and top with grated mozarella.

To each oyster, add a sliver of hot chili pepper and a small fresh parsley leaf to the heel end.

Grill until golden brown.

Serve hot.

Oysters go well with any quality wine, particularly a Pinot Gris.

Marcel Creurer
Silent Harvest Inc.

Duke's Oyster Appy

fresh oysters
seasoned flour
(can use any combination of salt, pepper,
paprika, seasoned salt, cayenne, garlic
powder)
egg, beaten
bread crumbs, crushed nacho chips
or crackers
garlic butter

Lightly poach as many oysters as you would like to make, just to make firm enough to handle.

Take out of shell and put shells aside for serving.

Let cool either overnight or if you are preparing immediately, put in ice bath until completely cooled.

Pat dry; roll in seasoned flour.

Dip in egg wash (beaten egg) and then coat with bread crumbs. You can change flavour and texture by using different types of bread or you can use crushed nacho chips or crackers.

Pan fry in garlic butter.

Serve back in shell.

"Dukelicious!"

Barrie Darnell, Mike Hnidy
Duke's Dockside Grill

"Spiked" Oysters

Oysters may be replaced with jumbo prawns and scallops.

6	large fresh oysters	6
3	cloves garlic, minced	3
1/4 cup	Spanish onions, fine dice	60 g
3 Tbsp	mushrooms, chopped	40 g
2 Tbsp	olive oil	30 mL
1 cup	whipping cream	250 mL
pinch	salt	pinch
pinch	white pepper	pinch
1 Tbsp	Brandy	15 mL
1 Tbsp	Ouzo	15 mL
3 oz	Reggiano cheese, finely grated	90 g

Shuck oysters and remove meat from shells. Reserve shell bottoms and rinse off. Refrigerate shells and oyster meat.

Heat a medium-sized skillet, add olive oil, mushrooms, onions and garlic. Sweat ingredients until onions are translucent, not brown.

Add both liquors, and flame off alcohol.

Place oysters in pan on medium heat. Cook 1 minute each side.

Add whipping cream. Bring to a slow simmer and reduce until the sauce achieves an olive oil consistency.

Place oysters back in the shell on baking tray. Spoon sauce over the oysters, filling the shell. Top with Reggiano cheese.

Broil oysters to achieve a golden brown surface.

Serve as an appetizer or as a meal with your favourite choice of starch and vegetables.

Chef Dennis Vaughan
Royal Coachman Pub and Catering

Oyster Misota

12	oysters on the half shell	12
1/2 cup	melted butter	125 mL
3	cloves garlic, minced	3
1/3 cup	cilantro, diced	75 mL
1 tsp	salt	5 mL
1/2 cup	white wine	125 mL
1 cup	sharp Cheddar cheese, shredded	250 mL

In a sauté pan, combine garlic, butter and white wine. Sauté 1 minute and add fresh cilantro.

Pour mixture generously on top of oysters.

Top with Cheddar cheese and bake at 350° F (180° C) until golden and bubbly.

Sean Frederickson
Shot in the Dark

Incredible Edibles from the Sea

We in Canada are very fortunate. We can now purchase very high quality Canadian made smoked oysters, processed without additives or oil. This gourmet product will tantalize your senses. After tasting just one, you will never want to settle for less.

smoked oysters, Canadian made gourmet
English cucumber
Goat cheese or other cream cheese
finely chopped chives

Slice English cucumber into rounds.

Spread Goat cheese or other cream cheese on one side of each cucumber round.

Place a small piece of smoked oyster on top of each cheese covered round.

Finish with finely chopped chives sprinkled on top.

Brent Petkau
Oysterman

Baked Oysters with Tomato, Parsley and Asiago Cheese

24	freshly shucked oysters in the half shell	24

Topping

5 or 6	ripe tomatoes, finely chopped	5 or 6
1/4 cup	parsley, finely chopped	60 mL
2 or 3	garlic cloves, finely chopped	2 or 3
3/4 cup	Asiago cheese, grated	175 mL
1/4 cup	olive oil	60 mL
	juice from 1 lemon	
	salt, white pepper and hot sauce, to taste	

Combine all the topping ingredients. Set aside.

Preheat oven to 450° F (230° C).

Place the oysters on a large baking sheet. Place a generous spoonful of topping on each oyster.

Bake for 12 to 15 minutes or until nicely browned.

Serve immediately. Enjoy!

Serves 4 as an appetizer

Brent Petkau
Oysterman

Oysters in Pernod Sauce

1 quart	fresh oysters	1 L
48 oz	clam nectar or fish stock	1.5 L
1/2	medium onion, finely diced	1/2
3 Tbsp	butter	45 mL
3 Tbsp	flour	45 mL
1 Tbsp	dry dill weed	15 mL
	or	
1/2 tsp	fresh dill, chopped	2 mL
	whipping cream	
	salt and pepper	
2 oz	Pernod	60 mL

Poach the oysters in boiling water only long enough to firm them. Remove and cool in refrigerator.

Heat stock or nectar to a boil for 10 minutes.

Sauté onion and dill in butter until onions soften. Remove from heat. Add flour to butter to make roux.

Pour hot stock into pot, put back on medium heat and whip until sauce thickens.

Cook out flour, then add cream to lighten and to taste.

Add Pernod. Mix and strain over oysters, then finish cooking oysters in the sauce.

Serve.

Fred Rose
Rose's Country Catering

Oysters with Champagne Sauce and Leeks

This recipe is intended to blow socks off and perhaps some other pieces of clothing as well. Truly divine indulgence!

36	small to medium-sized oysters with deep half shells	36
3/4 cup	heavy cream	175 mL
1 Tbsp	cornstarch	15 mL
1/4 cup	chopped leeks (the white portion of the leek)	60 mL
1/4 cup	chopped shallots	60 mL
4 Tbsp	unsalted butter	60 mL
1 cup	Champagne	250 mL
1 Tbsp	chopped pimiento	15 mL
1/2 tsp	celery salt	2 mL
1/4 tsp	white pepper	1 mL
1/8 tsp	Louisiana Hot Sauce	.5 mL
2 Tbsp	finely chopped parsley	30 mL
4	egg yolks	4
1 cup	grated white Cheddar cheese	250 mL
	(other types of white cheese also work well)	

In a small bowl, gradually whisk heavy cream into cornstarch. Set aside.

In a large skillet, lightly sauté leeks and shallots in butter over medium heat.

Stir in champagne, pimientos, celery salt, white pepper and hot pepper sauce. Bring to boil. Slowly whisk in cream mixture and parsley, bring to boil, whisking constantly.

Reduce heat. Whisk egg yolks in small bowl. Gradually whisk in 1/3 of hot sauce. Whisk yolk mixture into remaining sauce in skillet, mixing well. Remove from heat.

Preheat oven to 400° F (205° C). Arrange oysters on the deep half shells in shallow baking pan. Ladle some sauce over each oyster, being sure to cover oysters completely with sauce. Sprinkle with cheese.

Bake at 400° F (200° C) for 10 to 12 minutes, until oysters are opaque and sauce is bubbling.

If desired, broil briefly to brown tops.

Barely enough to serve 6

Brent Petkau
Oysterman

Calgary Oysters.

**small to medium-size oysters,
allow 2 to 3 per person
salt and pepper, to taste
garlic powder, to taste
onions, chopped
bacon bits
bread or cracker crumbs
butter**

Steam oysters open. Remove and discard the top shell.

Sprinkle each oyster with salt, pepper and garlic powder.

Smother each oyster in chopped onions and bacon bits.

Cover each oyster with bread or cracker crumbs.

Top each oyster with a dollop of butter.

Heat under the grill until golden brown.

Serve hot.

**Marcel Creurer
Silent Harvest Inc**

Riptide Chef's Favourite Oysters

12	fresh medium oysters	12
1 Tbsp	butter	15 mL
1	clove fresh garlic, minced	1
1	small shallot, finely chopped	1
1	fresh lemon	1
4 oz	candied salmon, chopped	125 mL
2 tsp	cracked black pepper	10 mL
1/2 cup	36% cream	125 mL
pinch	salt	pinch
1/2 cup	grated mozzarella cheese	125 mL
	lemon wedges	

First shuck the oysters and reserve in a bowl. Save the bottom shells to bake the oysters in.

In a pan, heat butter on medium heat and sauté minced garlic and shallots until golden. Squeeze in a tablespoon (15 mL) of fresh lemon juice to prevent the garlic from burning.

Add in chopped candied salmon and black pepper; sauté for a minute.

Add oysters to pan and sauté until they are cooked about half way.

Add cream and reduce by about a third. Season with a pinch of salt. By this time the oysters should be almost fully cooked.

Take off heat and place one oyster back into each shell and drizzle the remaining sauce evenly onto each oyster.

Top each oyster with grated mozzarella cheese and bake at 350° F (180° C) until cheese is melted and bubbling.

Arrange the finished oysters on a platter and garnish with wedges of lemon. Enjoy.

Chef Ryan Stewardson
Riptide Marine Pub

Sambuca Oysters

oysters
margarine
red onion, thinly sliced
Sambuca
whipping cream
salt and pepper, to taste
fresh tarragon

Melt margarine over medium-high heat. Add thinly sliced red onion. Sauté until half cooked.

Add Sambuca (watch for the flame) and when the "fire" is gone, pour in the whipping cream with some salt and pepper.

Reduce cream by one quarter, add oysters, reduce cream until thickened and oysters are cooked.

Garnish with fresh tarragon.

You can also make oysters and sauce separately and serve on the half shell with cream drizzled over.

Dawn Sturmey
Banners Restaurant

Wild Honey Mussels Sicilian Style

Great served as an appetizer, with garlic toast on the side for dipping, or serve tossed with your favourite pasta as a heartier meal.

2 lbs	B.C. Honey Mussels (other varieties such as Atlantic Blue will also work well)	1 kg
2 Tbsp	olive oil	30 mL
1	bulb fresh fennel, sliced	1
1	medium onion, sliced	1
4	cloves garlic, crushed	4
4	links spicy Italian sausage	4
1 cup	dry white wine	250 mL
14 oz	can diced tomatoes	398 mL
	fresh ground pepper, to taste	

Heat olive oil in your favourite stock pot. Add fennel, onions and garlic.

Sauté over medium heat until onions are transluscent. Add sausage and mussels.

Raise heat to high. Once sizzling, add wine and cover for 5 minutes.

Add diced tomatoes and pepper. Reduce heat and simmer 6 to 8 additional minutes.

Enjoy!

Kelley Lane
Fusilli Grill

Tom's Mussels

This leek sauce for mussels can be finished as either a cream or a tomato-based sauce. Either is delicious!

	mussels - enough to serve your party (2 lb/1 kg for 2 people)	
2	**leeks, chopped**	**2**
3	**cloves garlic, whole**	**3**
1/2 cup	**white wine**	**125 mL**
1/2 cup	**whipping cream**	**125 mL**
	OR	
1	**28 oz (796 mL) tin whole tomatoes, crushed**	**1**
	crushed chilies, if you want to spice it up	

Quickly fry leeks and garlic in oil (and chilies if desired).

Put in mussels, toss and cover for about 1 1/2 minutes.

Remove lid, put in white wine, cover and let mussels steam open.

Add either whipping cream or tomatoes, toss to mix.

Cover and let cream reduce or tomatoes heat through.

Serve immediately with a nice crusty bread.

Tom

Moules Munier

2 lbs	mussels, rinsed, drained and	1 kg
	debearded	
1 Tbsp	fresh crushed garlic	15 mL
1	medium onion, diced	1
1 Tbsp	fresh basil, chopped	15 mL
1 Tbsp	fresh thyme, chopped	15 mL
1 Tbsp	fresh rosemary, chopped	15 mL
3 Tbsp	olive oil	45 mL
2 Tbsp	butter	30 mL
1/2 cup	white wine, plus some to drink	125 mL
	Lawry's seasoned salt, to taste	
	white pepper, to taste	

Place butter and oil in a large heavy bottom frying pan. Heat on high and add garlic, onions, basil, thyme and rosemary.

Sauté 30 seconds and then add mussels with the seasoned salt and white pepper. Cover and allow to sauté for about 1 minute.

Add wine and cover again until the mussels open.

Remove from heat and serve immediately.

Serve with some French bread for dipping in the juices.

Serves 4

Chef David Larsen
The Chef's Kitchen

Mussel Delight

2 lbs	fresh local mussels	1 kg
2 Tbsp	olive oil	30 mL
1/4 cup	red onions, diced	60 mL
3 Tbsp	garlic, chopped	45 mL
	splash of white wine	
1/4 cup	whipping cream	60 mL
2 Tbsp	fresh chopped herbs	30 mL

In a large non-stick frying pan, add olive oil and heat until it is very hot. Add the onions and the garlic. Add the mussels, stirring until halfway cooked.

Add the white wine, deglazing the pan. Add the whipping cream and the fresh herbs, reducing until mussels are opened.

Remove from stove and spoon into a large serving bowl, garnish with lemon and parsley or whatever else you have to spare in your fridge.

If you are looking for a little more zip to your recipe, add a couple of tablespoons of salsa.

This recipe can be used with any shellfish.

A little reminder, when you are cooking seafood, do not overcook it; seafood should be juicy and tender.

Remember always to buy local when possible; fresh is best.

Chef Ken Guy
Beehive Seafood Grill and Cafe

Broiled Mussels on the Half Shell

Serve while hot for a great appetizer..

5	large blue mussels	5
3 cups	water	750 mL
4	cloves garlic, peeled	4
1/2	green onion, coarsely chopped	1/2
1/2	red pepper, coarsely chopped	1/2
1/2 cup	onion, coarsely chopped	125 mL
	juice of one lemon	
	(or 1 Tbsp/15 mL lemon concentrate)	
2 Tbsp	soy sauce	30 mL
1 tsp	sugar or honey	5 mL
	salt and pepper, to taste	
1 cup	grated Parmesan cheese	250 mL
1/4 cup	soft butter	60 mL

Steam mussels in water until open. Drain and remove meats; save the shells.

Mix garlic, green onion, red pepper, onion, lemon juice, soy sauce, sugar, salt, pepper, Parmesan cheese and butter well and blend in blender to coarse meal consistency.

Preheat the oven on broil and place the oven rack at the top of the oven under the broiler.

Place each mussel meat in half a mussel shell and arrange on a cookie sheet or large baking dish.

Sprinkle one teaspoon (5 mL) of spice mixture on top of each meat boat.

Broil only until light brown, about 10 minutes, watching carefully so they won't burn. Serve while hot and enjoy.

Xinh Dwelley
Taylor Shellfish Farms

Chipotle and Cream Mussels

2 lbs	Salt Spring Island mussels	1 kg
6	cloves garlic, peeled	6
1/4	bunch cilantro	1/4
1/2 tin	199 g chipotle peppers in adobo sauce	1/2 tin
6 Tbsp	butter	90 mL
6 Tbsp	flour	90 mL
3 cups	whipping cream	750 mL
	salt and pepper, to taste	

Purée the garlic, cilantro and chipotle peppers together.

Melt butter, add flour and mix. Cook for 2 minutes. Add whipping cream until well blended, about 3 minutes. Add salt and pepper to taste.

Add chipotle mix and stir another couple of minutes.

Add mussels and cook until shells open and mussels are firm and still plump, about 4 to 5 minutes on medium heat.

Divide into 4 separate bowls.

Serves 4

**Acme Food Co.
Nanaimo**

West Coast Mussels

1 1/2 lb	local mussels, cleaned	750 g
5	Roma tomatoes	5
3 - 4	shallots	3 - 4
4	cloves garlic, peeled	4
6 oz	hot smoked salmon	180 g
2 Tbsp	olive oil	30 mL
2 oz	Sambucca	60 mL
1 cup	white wine	250 mL
1 cup	fish stock	250 mL
3	green smoked jalapenos, chopped	3
1 cup	tomato sauce	250 mL
4 oz	feta cheese, for garnish (optional)	125 mL
4 oz	black olives, sliced, for garnish (optional)	125 mL

Finely dice Roma tomatoes, shallots, garlic and smoked salmon.

Warm pan at high heat. Sauté shallots in olive oil until clear. Add garlic, Sambuca, white wine and reduce by half.

Add mussels, chopped tomatoes and fish stock and reduce by half.

Add jalapenos, smoked salmon, tomato sauce and reduce to taste.

Garnish with feta cheese and olives before serving.

Serves 2

Ben Luck
Comfort Zone Foods

Scallops and Shrimp in White Wine

This is a great appetizer. Serve with a fresh baguette to mop up all the broth.

1 lb	scallops	450 g
1 lb	large shrimp, peeled and deveined	450 g
1/4 cup	flour, seasoned with salt and pepper	60 mL
1 Tbsp	extra virgin olive oil	15 mL
2 Tbsp	butter	30 mL
2	cloves garlic, minced	2
1	large shallot, minced	1
1/2 tsp	crushed red pepper flakes	2 mL
1 cup	dry white wine	250 mL
1 cup	chicken broth	250 mL
14 oz	can diced tomatoes in juice	397 g
1/4 tsp	saffron threads	1 mL
12	leaves fresh basil, shredded	12
1	lemon, zested	1

Lightly coat the scallops in flour seasoned with salt and pepper.

Preheat a large skillet over medium-high heat. Add the oil and butter. When the butter melts, add the scallops and brown for 2 minutes on each side. Remove from the pan and set aside.

Add a bit more oil to the pan and add the garlic, shallots and crushed red pepper flakes. Reduce the heat to medium and sauté the garlic and shallots for 2 minutes, stirring constantly.

Add wine to the pan and scrape up the pan drippings. Reduce the wine for 1 minute, then add stock, tomatoes and saffron.

When liquids come to a boil, add shrimp and cook 3 minutes. Return scallops to the pan and cook 2 to 3 minutes longer.

Transfer to a warm serving bowl and top with zest and basil.

Serves 4

Quality Foods

Scallops in Saffron Cream Sauce

1 lb	fresh scallops	500 g
1	egg yolk	1
pinch	saffron threads	pinch
1 Tbsp	boiling water	15 mL
3 oz	fresh Parmesan cheese, grated	90 g
1 1/2 Tbs	cream	25 mL
	salt and white pepper	
1/4 cup	butter	60 mL
3 Tbsp	whiskey or sherry	45 mL
	fresh dill and cherry tomatoes, to garnish	

Preheat oven to 400° F (200° C).

Clean scallops, separating roe and meat.

Place saffron in a small heatproof bowl, Pour boiling water over saffron, allow to cool, then squeeze threads well.

Crush roe of scallops to a paste using a mortar and pestle, fork, or blender. Add saffron, egg yolk, cheese, cream and season to taste with salt and pepper. Stir well to combine.

Melt butter, add scallops and cook over high heat for 1 minute, stirring constantly. Add whiskey and heat through.

Divide contents of pan between four individual serving dishes or scallop shells. Pour cream mixture over and bake for 20 minutes.

Served garnished with sprigs of dill and cherry tomatoes.

Serves 4

Amy Concepcion
Amy's Asian Foods & Cafe

Swimming Scallops or Mussels

48	swimming scallops or mussels	48
1 cup	white wine	250 mL
1/4 cup	celery and parsley	50 mL
6	green onions, chopped	6
1	garlic clove, sliced	1
1/4 cup	butter	60 mL

Place scallops or mussels in large skillet with tight lid.

Add wine, celery, parsley, green onions, garlic and butter.

Cook over quick heat until shells open.

Serve in bowls. Pour sauce over scallops or mussels.

Bob and Pat Martin
Patti Finn's Seafood

Dorchester Hotel Shellfish

2 lbs	shellfish (clams/mussels)	1 kg
1/2-3/4 c	white wine	125 - 175 mL
1/3 cup	whipping cream	75 mL
1 Tbsp	butter	15 mL
1/4 cup	onion, chopped	60 mL
1/4 cup	leek, julienne	60 mL
1	small tomato, diced	1
	salt and pepper, to taste	
3	leaves fresh basil, chopped	3

Heat pot, add onion, leek and butter. Sauté for 2 to 3 minutes.

Add shellfish and white wine. Let boil for 3 to 5 minutes until shellfish start to open.

Now add remaining ingredients. Let simmer for another 2 to 4 minutes, until shellfish completely open.

Scoop shellfish into bowl and pour liquid over. Sprinkle chopped basil over and serve.

Shawn Smith
Executive Chef
Best Western Dorchester Hotel
Nanaimo

Steamed Mussels or Clams

2 lbs	mussels or clams	1 kg
1/2	medium onion, finely diced	1/2
3	cloves garlic, crushed	3
1/4 cup	white wine	60 mL
1/2	lemon, squeezed	1/2
1/4 cup	water	60 mL
2 Tbsp	parsley, chopped	30 mL

If using clams, be sure to purge the clams before cooking.

Sauté onion, garlic and parsley together in large pot. After sweating for 3 minutes, add wine, water and lemon juice.

Add clams or mussels. Cover with tight lid and steam until they open, approximately 5 to 10 minutes.

Serve in large bowl and pour the liquid over the clams or mussels.

Fred Rose
Rose's Country Catering

Sambuca Clams

24	fresh Manilla clams	24
1/2 cup	vegetable stock	125 mL
1 cup	tomato juice	250 mL
1/2 cup	julienne vegetables	125 mL
1 tsp	garlic, minced	5 mL
1 tsp	shallots, finely chopped	5 mL
3 oz	Sambuca	90 mL
2 Tbsp	fresh herbs, chopped	30 mL
	salt and pepper	
2 Tbsp	butter	30 mL

Sauté julienne vegetables, garlic and shallots. Deglaze with vegetable stock, then add clams.

Add tomato sauce, Sambuca and fresh herbs. Cover and let simmer until all clams are open. Season with salt and pepper.

Before you plate this dish, add butter and mix in until the butter is just melted. This will give the dish a bright glossy look, while adding more flavour of the butter.

Chef Shawn Gardiner
April Point Lodge

Shrimp Mousse

1 cup	shrimp	250 mL
1/2 cup	onion, finely chopped	125 mL
1/4 cup	green pepper, finely chopped	60 mL
1	envelope unflavoured gelatin	1
1	8 oz (284 mL) can tomato soup	284 mL
1	8 oz (225 g) package Philadelphia cream cheese	1
1/2 cup	mayonnaise	125 mL
1/2 cup	water	125 mL

Dissolve gelatin in water. Melt cheese in soup; be careful not to boil. Add gelatin and cool.

Combine onion, pepper and shrimp with mayonnaise. Add cold soup mixture and put in mold.

Serve with a variety of crackers or tortilla chips.

Sandy Tracy

Fish Bait

12	jumbo prawns, peeled and deveined	12
12	mussels	12
12	swimming scallops	12
20	pieces cubed halibut or salmon or both	20
2 Tbsp	olive oil	30 mL
1/4 cup	red onions, diced	60 mL
2 Tbsp	garlic, chopped	30 mL
1/4 cup	medium salsa	60 mL
1/4 cup	white wine	60 mL
1/4 cup	whipping cream	60 mL

In a large non-stick frying pan, add the olive oil and heat until it is very hot. Add the onions and garlic. Add the halibut and/or salmon, stirring until halfway cooked. Then add the white wine, deglazing the pan.

Add the prawns, mussels, and scallops. Add the salsa and finish with the whipping cream, reducing until the mussels and scallops have opened.

Remove from stove and spoon into a large serving bowl. Garnish with lemon and parsley or whatever you have to spare in your fridge.

A little reminder, when you are cooking seafood, do not overcook it; seafood should be juicy and tender.

Remember always to buy local when possible; fresh is best.

Serves 4 as an appetizer or serves 2 as a main dish.

Chef Ken Guy
Beehive Seafood Grill and Cafe

Ceviche

1 lb	peeled fresh prawns	500 g
3/4 lb	scallops	375 g
1 Tbsp	olive oil	15 mL
4	limes	4
1/2 cup	red onion, finely chopped	125 mL
	salt and pepper to taste	
1/2 cup	cilantro, finely chopped	125 mL

Two hours before serving, butterfly and devein prawns. Cut each scallop in 6 pieces.

Squish cut lime halves over seafood, washing hands after every lime, so not to add the bitter of rind.

Just before serving, add cilantro and onion. Salt and pepper to taste.

Enjoy.

Serve with Fresh Salsa Spritz.

Bianca Haines
Wacko Taco

Fresh Salsa Spritz

6	firm Roma tomatoes	6
2 Tbsp	processed garlic	30 mL
8	stems of cilantro	8
1	lime	1
1	lemon	1
	pinch of salt	

Cut tomatoes into slices, then cut them into long small strips, then crossways, ending up with small cubes.

Add processed garlic.

Squeeze half a lemon and half a lime over tomatoes and garlic in bowl.

Take leaves of cilantro, finely chop, and add to the bowl.

Squeeze remaining half of lemon and half of lime. Stir in.

Add pinch of salt.

Let stand 5 minutes. Enjoy.

Serve with Ceviche and tacos or crackers. Serve immediately after preparing Ceviche.

Jane Labbe
Wacko Taco

Surprise Spread

Crab meat also works well in this appetizer.

2 - 3	4 oz (113 g) cans of broken shrimp, drained	2 - 3
8 oz	cream cheese, softened	250 g
1/2 cup	sour cream	125 mL
1/4 cup	mayonnaise	60 mL
1 cup	seafood cocktail sauce	250 mL
2 cups	shredded mozzarella cheese	500 mL
1	green pepper, chopped	1
3	green onions, chopped	3
1	tomato, diced	1

Mix cream cheese, sour cream and mayonnaise together; spread over 12 inch (30 cm) pizza pan. Scatter shrimp over cheese mixture.

Add layers of seafood sauce, mozzarella cheese, green pepper, onions, and tomato.

Cover and chill until ready to serve.

Supply assorted crackers for spreading; or tortilla chips.

Crab meat may be substituted for shrimp.

Serves 8 to 10

Bertha Seabolt

Oyster Stew

6 - 8	fresh oysters, shucked, liquor saved	6 - 8
1 cup	milk	250 mL
1 or 2	egg yolks	1 or 2
1/4 cup	cream	60 mL

nutmeg
salt
white pepper

In a saucepan, cook oysters in their own juice and milk until done, no longer than 5 minutes.

Take the egg yolks and mix with the cream. Add some of the hot liquid and blend in a cup. Return all to the stew.

Add a touch of nutmeg, salt and white pepper to taste.

Serve..

Originally from Willa Budge

West Coast Fish and Prawn Stew

1/2 lb	prawns	250 g
1 lb	halibut or monkfish or any white fish with firm flesh	500 g
2 Tbsp	vegetable oil	30 mL
1	clove garlic, chopped	1
1	red bell pepper, seeded, cored and sliced into thin strips	1
1	green bell pepper, seeded, cored and sliced into thin strips	1
1	small carrot, grated	1
1	medium onion, sliced	1
2 cups	cubed tomatoes	500 mL
1	bay leaf	1
1 tsp	ground cumin	5 mL
2 Tbsp	chopped fresh parsley	30 mL
1/2 cup	white wine	125 mL
1 cup	fish stock	250 mL
1 tsp	salt	5 mL
2	potatoes, peeled and sliced 1 inch (2.5 cm) thick	2

In a large Dutch oven or saucepan, heat oil. Add garlic, bell peppers, carrot and onion. Cook for 2 minutes. Then stir in the tomatoes and cook for another minute.

Add the fish, prawns and bay leaf to the vegetables. Add cumin and parsley. Pour in the white wine, fish stock and season to taste with salt. Cover and bring the liquid to a boil.

Add the potatoes, cover the pan again and cook for 15 minutes or until the potatoes, fish and prawns are cooked thoroughly. Remove the bay leaf and discard.

Spoon the solid ingredients into serving bowls, then top with the liquid and fresh chopped parsley.

Serve with your favourite homemade bread. Serves 4.

Chef Dwight Walden
North Island College Cook Training Program

Cacciucco or Fish Stew

This is a traditional Tuscan dish, the choice of the fish that goes into the dish is up to the cook.

In Livorno Tuscany, a peculiarity of the preparation of Cacciucco is to put a stone from the bottom of the sea into the bottom of the pot. This is believed to enhance the flavour and to impress Neptune to overlook the theft of the various ingredients from his kingdom.

This dish is thought to come from an Athenian recipe. Even without the stone in the pot, it is delicious, although the stone does add a bit of romance to this dish. It won't hurt anyone and is playful and fun to bring out to show your guests.

1 lb	mussels, remove the beards by pulling from the top to the hinge and rinse in cold water	500 g
1 lb	clams, rinse in cold water	500 g
1 lb	prawns, peeling is your choice, its messy not to peel, but fun	500 g
1 lb	nice white fish, halibut or rock cod	500 g
1/2	red onion, minced	1/2
2	cloves garlic, minced (the best garlic is the variety with the red stripes)	2
1	small bunch Italian flat parsley, minced	1
4 Tbsp	good virgin olive oil	60 mL
1 lb	vine ripe tomatoes or 1 large can plum tomatoes (if the tomatoes are fresh, blanch and peel)	500 g
2 Tbsp	balsamic vinegar diluted in 3/4 cup (175 mL) white wine	30 mL
	a pinch of crumbled dried red peppers	
	a pinch of sea salt	
	good sour dough italian bread, toasted and rubbed with garlic	

Make sure that your shellfish are tightly closed and kept on ice until you are ready to drop them in the pot. Keep the clams and mussels separate, you will add them to the pot in layers.

Sauté the onion, parsley and garlic in the olive oil in a deep bottomed pot.

Once the onion has turned translucent, stir in the chopped tomatoes. When the tomatoes are done, stir in the vinegar and wine.

Blend in a processor or a hand held puréer, return to the stove. Add a few more tablespoons of olive oil if you like.

Add the fish in layers. Add the clams first, cover with the lid. The shells are thicker and will take 2 minutes longer to cook, then add the mussels, prawns and white fish. Cover with the lid and cook just until the clams and mussels are open and the prawns are pink and the fish is firm and white. The white fish will cook quickly if cut into small pieces.

Place the bread in the bottom of a large soup bowl. Ladle the fish stew over the bread. If you get the stone, just give it back to the cook and thank Neptune.

Serve with a choice of a red or white dry wine. Toast your loved ones and give thanks for the clean waters that grow and nourish this wonderful shellfish. Enjoy.

Serves 4

Continue to double the recipe for more people.

Silky Pearce
Silky's Bed and Breakfast

Seafood Chiopino

2 lb	fresh clams	1 kg
2 lb	fresh mussels	1 kg
1 lb	local prawns	500 g
1 lb	fresh scallops	500 g
2 lb	crab legs	1 kg
1 lb	desired fish (salmon, halibut, cod, etc.) cut in 1 inch (2.5 cm) pieces	500 g
1/4 cup	olive oil	50 mL
1	recipe Tomato Saffron Broth	1
1/2	bunch parsley, chopped for garnish lemon wedges, for garnish	1/2

In a large pot with a lid, heat oil and sauté fish, prawns and scallops for 2 minutes. Add tomato saffron broth and shellfish. Cover and let steam 5 to 7 minutes, until shellfish opens.

Remove from heat and serve in bowls with shellfish around the edge and crab legs on top. Sprinkle with parsley.

Tomato Saffron Broth

1	medium onion, cut julienne	1
1/2	fennel bulb, cut julienne	1/2
2	stocks celery, cut julienne	2
3	cloves garlic, chopped	3
1/4 cup	olive oil	50 mL
1/2 cup	white wine	125 mL
1/4 cup	lemon juice	60 mL
1/3 tsp	Spanish saffron	2-3 g
2 cups	whole plum tomatoes with juice	500 mL
1 cup	tomato juice	250 mL
2 oz	Sambuca	60 mL

In a heavy bottomed pot, sauté onions, fennel, celery and garlic with the olive oil. When the vegetables are opaque, deglaze with white wine and lemon juice, reduce by one quarter. Add tomatoes and simmer until sauce coats the back of a spoon; add Sambuca.

Kerry Kupser
Salmon Point Restaurant and Bar

April Point Seafood Hotpot

8	fresh local mussels	8
8	fresh Manilla clams	8
8	bay scallops	8
2 oz	Vancouver Island salmon	60 g
2 oz	halibut	60 g
4 oz	julienne vegetables	125 mL
1 tsp	garlic	5 mL
1 tsp	shallots	5 mL
2 oz	white wine	60 mL
10 oz	tomato sauce	310 mL
6 oz	vegetable stock	180 mL
2	garlic rubbed croutons	2
2 oz	roasted red peppers thinly sliced (if not available, any type is fine)	60 mL

Sauté julienne vegetables, garlic and shallots. Deglaze with white wine, then add all seafood.

Add tomato sauce and vegetable stock. Cover and let simmer until all shellfish are open.

Serve in two large bowls, with rice. Garnish with a garlic rubbed crouton and the red pepper sauce.

Garlic Rubbed Croutons
Take a piece of bread and cut a 4 inch (10 cm) diameter circle. Spread with garlic butter and bake in low oven until lightly golden.

Roasted Red Pepper Sauce
Place red peppers in 425° F (220° C) oven. Bake until a dark colour. Cover with plastic wrap and let stand for 15 minutes. Peel all skin and deseed, then place in food processor. Season well.

Serves 2

Chef Shawn Gardiner
April Point Lodge

Seafood Hotpot

You can use any combination of seafood for this Hotpot.

6	mussels	6
6	clams	6
1/2	Dungeness crab, segmented	1/2
4	sea scallops	4
4	large prawns	4
6	swimming scallops (pink shells)	6
4 oz	halibut, cut in large cubes	120 g
4 oz	salmon, cut in large cubes	120 g
4 cups	roast red pepper tomato sauce (see recipe)	1L
3 oz	leeks, julienne	85 g
1 Tbsp	fresh chilies, finely chopped	15 mL

Place all ingredients in a large saucepan. Bring to a simmer. Gently shuffle ingredients, then cover.

Cook for 10 to 12 minutes or until shellfish have completely opened.

Place in large flared soupbowls and serve with hot crisp rolls.

Serves 2

Chef Dennis Vaughan
Royal Coachman Pub and Catering

Roast Red Pepper Tomato Sauce with Saffron and Pernod

This base sauce can be used for any seafood or chicken. Serve with your favourite pasta.

11.5 oz	tin roast red peppers	340 mL
11.5 oz	tin tomato filets	340 mL
5.5 oz	tin tomato paste	156 mL
7/8 cup	water	200 mL
1/2 cup	olive oil	125 mL
1/2 cup	crushed garlic	125 mL
1/4 cup	sugar	60 g
4 tsp	salt	20 g
2 tsp	pepper	10 g
2 Tbsp	paprika	30 g
3	bay leaves	3
1 tsp	seasoning salt	5 g
12	strands saffron	12
1/4 cup	white wine	50 mL
2 tsp	Pernod	10 mL
1	small cinnamon stick	1

Remove peppers from the tin, keep liquid, and cut in 1 1/4 inch (3 cm) chunks.

Place roast peppers and liquid in saucepan. Add tomato filets, tomato paste, water, olive oil, garlic, sugar, salt, pepper, paprika, bay leaves and seasoning salt.

Bring to a full boil and simmer 15 minutes.

Add saffron, white wine, Pernod and cinnamon stick and simmer an additional 5 minutes. Remove cinnamon stick.

Chef Dennis Vaughan
Royal Coachman Pub and Catering

Cioppino or Bouillabaisse

	clams - in shells	
	uncooked crab - in shells	
	oysters - in shells	
	white fish - cod or halibut	
	salmon	
2	onions, chopped	2
8 - 10	cloves garlic, chopped	8 - 10
1	green pepper, chopped	1
1	red pepper, chopped	1
1	stalk celery, chopped	1
1 cup	parsley, finely chopped	250 mL
2	large tins tomato juice	2
28 oz	tin stewed tomatoes	796 mL
1 Tbsp	oregano	15 mL
1 Tbsp	basil	15 mL
1 Tbsp	thyme	15 mL
1 Tbsp	tarragon	15 mL
3	bay leaves	3
3 Tbsp	sugar	45 mL
2-3 cups	white wine	500 - 750 mL
1	can beer (or more)	1

Using a heavy large cooking pot, sauté in oil slowly the onions, garlic, green pepper, red pepper and celery. When onion starts to turn clear, add chopped parsley and sauté for a few minutes.

Add tomato juice, stewed tomatoes, oregano, basil, thyme, tarragon, bay leaves and sugar. Let simmer for 1 to 2 hours, being careful not to burn on the bottom. Then add white wine and beer and simmer a bit longer.

Scrub the clams, break up the uncooked crab after cleaning. Layer the clams in the sauce, then layer the crab and simmer for 8 minutes until the clams start to open. Then add layer of oysters in the shell (also scrubbed first) and simmer for a few more minutes. Add layer of white fish, such as cod or halibut and salmon. Simmer very carefully until the cod and salmon are just firmed Serve with hot French garlic bread.

Bertha Seabolt

Seafood Ragout

2 cups	baby shrimp	500 mL
1 cup	mussels (no shell)	250 mL
1 cup	scallops (no shell)	250 mL
1/2 cup	Manilla clams (no shell)	125 mL
1	white onion, diced	1
3	large carrots, diced	3
2	celery stalks, diced	2
2 Tbsp	minced garlic	30 mL
1 Tbsp	Dijon mustard	15 mL
1 cup	flour	250 mL
4 cups	fumet (fish stock)	1 L
1/2 lb	butter	250 g
4 cups	heavy cream	1 L
	salt and pepper	
	puff pastry (vulovant shells)	
	fiddleheads sautéed in brandy	
	(for garnish)	

Sauté the celery, carrot, and onion in the butter. Add flour to form a roux. At this point make sure you cook the flour with the vegetables until it starts to lightly change to golden colour.

Slowly add the fish stock. Remember with roux, if its hot, then the liquid must be cool. Do not add hot liquid to a hot roux; you will get lumps.

Add the seafood, garlic and Dijon mustard. Cook for about 30 minutes.

Add any other seasonings, and the heavy cream.

Bake the puff pastry shells.

Serve the ragout in shells. Garnish with a few fiddleheads sautéed in brandy.

Chef Shawn Gardiner
April Point Lodge

Clam Chowder

2	5 oz (142 g) tins baby clams	2
2	8 oz (240 mL) tins clam nectar	2
4 oz	chopped bacon or salt pork	120 g
1	10 oz (284 mL) tin chicken broth or consommé	1

1 1/2 cup	potatoes, diced	375 mL
1	onion, chopped	1
3/4 cup	celery, chopped	175 mL
3/4 cup	carrots, chopped	175 mL
3/4 cup	green or red pepper, chopped	175 mL
3/4 cup	mushrooms, sliced	175 mL
1	28 oz (796 mL) tin stewed tomatoes	1
1 - 2 cup	whipping cream	250 - 500 mL
1 1/2 tsp	Worcestershire sauce	7 mL
	few cloves garlic, chopped finely	
2	bay leaves	2
1/2 tsp	dry mustard	2 mL
1/2 tsp	sugar	2 mL
2 tsp	parsley	10 mL
1/2 tsp	thyme	2 mL
	salt and pepper	

Brown the bacon or salt pork, add carrots, celery, onion and potato. Brown some more, then add green pepper and mushrooms and cook all these lightly.

Add baby clams with liquid and let boil. Add clam nectar and chicken broth or consommé and the tomatoes.

Add Worcestershire sauce, garlic, bay leaves, dry mustard, sugar and parsley. Let simmer a bit longer. Season to taste with salt and pepper. If you would like to add more baby clams in the chowder, add them now. When all vegetables are almost done, add the whipping cream and heat through.

For an added touch, scrub fresh clams in the shells and add to the chowder at the last few moments to let them cook.
Serve with a heated baguette or French garlic bread.

Bertha Seabolt

Clam Miso Soup

24	clams	24
4 cups	water	1 L
1/2 cup	katsuobushi (dried bonito flakes)	125 mL
3 Tbsp	miso paste	45 mL
1/4 cup	green onions, chopped	60 mL

Put the water in a pan and heat on medium heat. Just before the water boils, add the katsuobushi. When the water boils, stop the heat and strain the broth. Japanese call this broth "Dashi".

Put the Dashi in a pan and bring to a boil.

Put the clams in boiled Dashi. Wait until the clams open.

Scoop out some Dashi from the pan and dissolve miso paste in it. Then return that to the pan. Do not boil the soup after you put miso in it.

Stop the heat and add chopped green onion.

Makes 4 servings

Keiko Kakubari
Katie's Rice Box

Crab Soup

3 1/2 lb	crab	1.5 kg
1	carrot, sliced	1
2	onions, thinly sliced	2
1 cup	white wine	250 mL
7 Tbsp	long grain rice	105 mL
	salt and pepper	
	croutons to serve	

Put carrots and onion in a pan with wine, salt and pepper and 1 quart (1 L) of water. Bring to a boil and simmer for 20 minutes.

Meanwhile put the rice in salted boiling water and simmer for 15 minutes. Drain.

Wash the crab in plenty of cold water. Plunge them into bouillon. Bring it back to a boil and then simmer for 5 minutes.

Using a slotted spoon, remove the crabs from the pan and grind the meat in a food processor. Strain the puree, pressing it well and return it to the bouillon.

Add the rice and bring the soup to the boil once more.

Adjust seasonings and serve with tiny croutons.

Linda McRoberts
Iron Kettle

Shrimp and Scallop Gumbo
(without the heat)

8 oz	shrimp	250 g
12	large scallops	12
1	red pepper, chopped	1
1	green pepper, chopped	1
3	stalks celery, chopped	3
1	onion, diced	1
2	cloves garlic, diced	2
1	14 oz (425 mL) tin tomato sauce	1
2 - 3 Tbs	sour cream	30 - 45 mL
1/2 tsp	oregano	2 mL
1 tsp	chili powder	5 mL

Preheat oven to 350° F (180° C).

In a large frying pan, sauté green and red peppers, celery, onion and garlic quickly in oil.

Add scallops and sear for 1 minute each side.

Add tomato sauce, chili powder and oregano. Once tomato sauce is heated through, add sour cream and stir in.

Again let it heat through and then add shrimp.

Heat for 1 minute and then transfer the whole contents into a casserole dish. Cover and place in the oven for at least 20 minutes, but longer if possible, up to 40 minutes or so. (The oven makes the flavour better).

Serve over rice.

Tom

Grilled Prawn Caesar Salad

6	large prawns	6
	lemon juice	
	garlic	
3 cups	Romaine lettuce, chopped	750 mL
3	slices bacon, cooked crisp and crumbled	3
1/4 cup	Parmesan cheese, grated	60 mL
1/2 cup	good quality bottled Caesar dressing	125 mL
	croutons	

Grill or sauté large peeled and deveined prawns in lemon juice and garlic until pink and lightly browned.

Toss the lettuce, bacon, Parmesan cheese, Caesar dressing and croutons together. Turn out onto plate.

Top with grilled prawns.

Serves 1

Dick's Fish and Chips

West Coast Seafood Salad

4 each	prawns, peeled and deveined	4 each
4 each	scallops	4 each
5 each	mussels, beards removed and scrubbed	5 each
1	lemon wedge	1
2 cups	Romaine lettuce, chopped	500 mL
2 cups	Spring mix lettuce	500 mL
6 slices	cucumber	6 slices
6	cherry tomatoes	6
1	carrot, shredded	1
1/4	red pepper, sliced	1/4
1/4	green pepper, sliced	1/4
2 Tbsp	Balsamic vinegar	30 mL
4 Tbsp	butter, melted	60 mL
pinch	black pepper	pinch
pinch	thyme leaves	pinch
pinch	dill weed	pinch
1	clove fresh garlic, minced	1
1 oz	white wine	30 mL

Sauté the shellfish in butter briefly. Add garlic and herbs. When the garlic is sizzling, add wine.

Cover and simmer for 3 to 5 minutes, until seafood is no longer opaque.

Arrange lettuce and vegetables on serving plate.

Remove shellfish from butter sauce and arrange over vegetables.

Add vinegar to butter sauce and drizzle over entire salad while still warm.

Serve with lemon wedge..

Chef Scott Hamel
Tsa-Kwa-Luten Lodge & RV Park

Spanakopita Wrap

	shrimp, crab, salmon or tuna	
1 lb	package filo pastry	454 g
3	cloves garlic	3
pinch	fresh dill	pinch
2	eggs	2
1	green pepper, diced	1
1	onion, diced	1
4 oz	herbed cream cheese	125 mL
8 oz	nacho cheese	250 mL
1/2 Tbsp	crushed peppers	8 mL
12 oz	frozen spinach, chopped, drained or fresh spinach	650 g

Sauté onions and peppers. Add drained spinach. Add garlic, dill, eggs, shellfish, cream cheese, nacho cheese and crushed peppers. Mix all together.

Unwrap filo pastry (keep covered with a damp cloth). Use 3 pieces of filo per wrap.

Oil the filo pastry lightly, lay out filo pastry on counter diagonally, put mixture in the middle. Roll pastry over mixture, tuck in the sides, finish rolling to the end.

Bake at 350° F (180° C) for 20 to 25 minutes until golden brown.

Patti Burley
Plaza Bakery

Sundance Oyster Wrap

This sumptuous and nutritious wrap is a fast and easy meal to make. We use local fresh oysters from Cortes Island, and our customers keep coming back for more!

3	large oysters	3
1 Tbsp	vegetable oil	15 mL
1/4 tsp	lemon pepper	1 mL
pinch	cayenne	pinch
1	egg	1
1/4 cup	flour	60 mL
12 inch	tomato tortilla wrap	30 cm
2	slices crisp bacon	2
2 Tbsp	cream cheese (more or less, to taste	30 mL
1 Tbsp	tartar sauce	15 mL
1	carrot, shredded or "stringed"	1
	red or green peppers, diced	
	red and/or green onions, sliced	
	handful of lettuce	

Put vegetable oil in frying pan, and heat. Mix flour and cayenne together. Beat egg. Dip oysters into egg, then into flour/cayenne mixture to coat. Sauté oysters in hot oil for at least 3 minutes on each side.

While oysters are sautéing, spread the cream cheese on the tortilla wrap. Make sure the entire wrap has cream cheese and then crumble the bacon slices over the tortilla wrap.

When oysters are cooked, place in a row, near bottom third of tortilla wrap. Spread tartar sauce on oysters. Sprinke lemon pepper over oysters. Then build your wrap with the vegetables, onions, peppers, carrot strings and lettuce.

Fold two sides of wrap toward the centre, and start rolling at bottom of wrap. Roll wrap tightly as you go. The cream cheese at the end of the wrap will hold the wrap together. Voila! Enjoy!

Sundance Java Bar

Shrimp and Avocado Wrap

1/2 cup	canned or fresh shrimp (cooked)	125 g
1	12 in (30 cm) flour tortilla	1
1 oz	soft cream cheese	30 mL
1 cup	Romaine lettuce, chopped	250 mL
1/2 cup	tomato, diced	125 mL
2 Tbsp	salad dressing of your choice (optional)	30 mL
	salt and pepper, to taste	

Spread flour tortilla with cream cheese (in a rectangle in the centre).

In a small bowl, combine shrimp, lettuce, tomato, salad dressing, salt and pepper, and pile them on the cream cheese.

With the long side of the rectangle horizontal to you, fold the bottom over the pile. Bring in the ends to the centre and roll the tortilla away from you.

Cut diagonally and serve with carrot and celery sticks.

The Uphill Grind

Grilled Oyster Burger

3 - 4	oysters	3 - 4
2 Tbsp	chopped onion	30 mL
	fresh lemon juice	
1	Kaiser bun, lightly toasted	1
	Tartar sauce	
	lettuce	
	tomato	

In a non-stick pan, sauté oysters and onion in fresh lemon juice for about 4 minutes per side, or until lightly browned.

Place onions on a lightly toasted Kaiser bun that has been spread with Tartar sauce.

Top with oysters, lettuce and tomato. Serve.

Serves 1

Dick's Fish and Chips

Crab Cakes with Pineapple Papaya Salsa

8 oz	crab meat	225 g
6 Tbsp	cream (35%)	90 mL
2 Tbsp	red bell pepper, small dice	30 g
2 Tbsp	green bell pepper, small dice	30 g
	clarified butter, as needed	
1/2	bunch green onions, diced	1/2
6 Tbsp	fresh breadcrumbs	90 g
	salt and pepper, to taste	
1 1/2 tsp	Dijon mustard	7 mL
	Worcestershire sauce, to taste	
	Tabasco sauce, to taste	
1	egg, beaten	1

Place the cream in a saucepan and bring to a boil. Reduce by half. Chill the cream well.

Sauté the red and green pepper in a small amount of clarified butter until tender.

Combine the crab meat, reduced cream, peppers, green onions and 3 tablespoons (45 g) of the breadcrumbs along with salt, pepper, Dijon mustard, Worcestershire sauce, Tabasco sauce and egg. Mix all ingredients.

Using a round mold, form the crab cakes into desired size.

Place the crab cakes into remaining breadcrumbs.

Heat a sauté pan over moderate heat and add enough clarified butter to cover the bottom of the pan.

Add the crab cakes to the pan and cook until done, turning only once, until they are golden brown. Remove and drain on absorbent paper.

Serve the crab cakes with the Pineapple Papaya Salsa.

Makes 8 - 2 oz (60 g) crab cakes. 4 servings

Pineapple Papaya Salsa

1 cup	tomatoes	225 g
1	fresh pineapple, use only 1/2	1
1	fresh papaya, use only 1/2	1
1/2	bunch green onions, sliced	1/2
1/2	bunch fresh cilantro	1/2
1	jalapeno, seeded, minced	1
1 1/2 Tbs	lemon juice	25 mL
1/2 -1 tsp	garlic, chopped	2 - 5 g
1 tsp	salt	5 g

Core and dice the tomatoes.

Peel and dice the pineapple.

Peel, seed and dice the papaya.

Combine all ingedients and chill.

Yield: 4 cups (1 litre)

Chef Dwight Walden
North Island College
Cook Training Program

Sushi Made Easy.

Rice

2 cups	Japanese rice	500 mL
2 1/2 cup	water	750 mL
2 Tbsp	seasoned rice vinegar	30 mL

Rinse rice under cold water 4 or 5 times. Let dry.

Cook rice and water on medium for 10 minutes. Turn to high until boiling, then back to medium-low for 10 to 15 minutes.

When rice is cooked, cover with a clean damp cloth and let stand for 15 minutes.

Mix rice in a large non-metal bowl with seasoned rice vinegar, and let cool.

This makes enough rice for 8 rolls

Shrimp Roll

shrimp
avocado
sprouts
Japanese Mayonnaise

California Roll

crab meat
flying fish roe
cucumber
avocado
Japanese mayonnaise

Campbell River Roll

crab meat
salmon
flying fish roe
cucumber
avocado
Japanese mayonnaise

Place a sheet of nori onto a bamboo mat. Spread sushi rice on top of the nori and flatten to 1/4 inch (.5cm). Leave at least a 1/2 inch (1.25 cm) strip clear at the top edge..

Place a line of Japanese mayonnaise across the rice. Place about 3 to 4 tablespoons (45 - 60 mL) of ingredients (depending upon which type of roll you are preparing) on the rice in a straight line. Leave about 1 inch (2.5 cm) away from the bottom edge of the nori.

Slightly wet the top edge of the nori. Roll tightly from bottom to the top edge, with the help of the bamboo mat.

Cut into 6 to 8 equal pieces. Repeat for other rolls.

Serve with wasabi and soy sauce on the side..

Heidi Jochimski
Susi's Seafoods

Oyster Stuffing for Turkey

This recipe will make enough stuffing for a 14 to 16 lb turkey

2 pints	oysters, any size	1 L
1 lb	sausage meat (regular or Italian)	500 g
4 1/2 cup	celery, chopped	1 L
2 cups	onion, chopped	500 mL
1 cup	slivered almonds	250 mL
3	eggs	3
2	7.5 oz (210 g) packages stuffing mix	2
1 1/2 - 2 cups chicken broth		375-500 mL

Basting

1/2 cup	butter	125 mL
1 - 2	cloves garlic, chopped	1 - 2
1 tsp	salt	5 mL
1 tsp	pepper	5 mL
1 tsp	sage	5 mL
pinch	sugar	pinch

Cook sausage until well done. Drain well. Add celery and onion, cook until tender.

Blanch oysters 2 to 3 minutes. Cut to bite-size.

Add stuffing mix, eggs, chicken broth and oysters. Remove from heat and mix until crumbs are moist. Stuff turkey with mixture.

For basting, melt butter and add garlic. Sauté until golden. Add salt, pepper, sage and sugar. Remove from heat.

Mix all ingredients thoroughly. Baste turkey with mixture.

Cover and bake turkey at 350° F (180 ° C) for 3 hours, or until done. Baste occasionally during cooking. During the last 30 minutes of cooking, remove lid. This will brown the skin.

Xinh Dwelley
Taylor Shellfish Farms

Entrées

Spicy Prawn Sauté with Basmati Rice Pilaf

1 lb	fresh or frozen prawns	500 g
1 Tbsp	lemon juice	15 mL
2 Tbsp	Cajun spice	30 mL
1/2 tsp	Tabasco sauce	2 mL
1 Tbsp	Worcestershire sauce	15 mL
2	cloves fresh garlic	2
1/4 cup	olive oil	60 mL
	salt and pepper to taste	
1 cup	Basmati rice	250 mL
2 cups	water	500 mL
1/4 cup	olive oil	60 mL
2	cloves fresh garlic	2
1 tsp	salt	5 mL
1/2 tsp	black pepper	2 mL

In a stock pot, boil the rice, water, olive oil, garlic, salt and pepper together. When it starts to boil, turn the heat to low. Let the rice simmer for 10 to 15 minutes.

In a skillet, heat the olive oil. Put the prawns, lemon juice, Cajun spice, Tabasco sauce, Worcestershire sauce, garlic, salt and pepper all together in the skillet.

Cook them on high heat. Keep mixing them.

When the prawns turn pink, they are ready to serve.

Serve prawns on the rice pilaf.

Serves 4 to 5

Surinder Tsangaris
White Tower Restaurant

Prawns with Cashew Nuts

12	prawns	12
2 Tbsp	canola oil	30 mL
1 tsp	minced garlic	5 mL
1 Tbsp	fish sauce	15 mL
1 Tbsp	oyster sauce	15 mL
1 Tbsp	Maggi seasoning	15 mL
1/4 cup	chicken stock	60 mL
1/2	red onion, sliced	1/2
1/2	red pepper, sliced	1/2
1/2	green peper, sliced	1/2
	broccoli, chopped in large chunks	
1/2 cup	cashews	125 mL
	ground black pepper, to taste	

Heat oil in pan on high. Add garlic.

Add prawns, red onion, red and green peppers, broccoli and cashews.

Add fish sauce, oyster sauce, maggi and chicken stock. Stir-fry on high for 1 minute.

Sprinkle with ground black pepper and serve.

Auttawee Mongkolsute
Baan Thai Restaurant

Wild Mushroom Risotto with Prawns

30 - 36	large prawns	30 - 36
2 oz	dried Porcini mushrooms	60 g
1 lb	mixed fresh wild mushrooms	500 g
	such as Chanterelles, Oyster, etc.	
4 Tbsp	extra virgin olive oil	60 mL
4	garlic cloves, finely chopped	4
4 Tbsp	unsalted butter	60 g
1	onion, finely chopped	1
1	small carrot, finely chopped	1
1	leek, finely chopped	1
1 1/2 cup	Arborio rice	375 g
5-6 cups	chicken broth	1.25 - 1.5 L
1/2 cup	grated Parmesan Reggianno	125 g
6 Tbsp	flat leaf parsley, finely chopped	90 g
1/4 cup	Vermouth	60 mL

Cover dried mushrooms with boiling water and set aside for about 30 minutes; then strain.

Heat 3 tablespoons (45 mL) of the olive oil in a large pan and add the fresh mushrooms. Cook on high heat, stirring for about 2 minutes, then add the garlic and the soaked mushrooms. Cook for another 2 minutes, then set aside.

Heat the rest of the oil and a small amount of the unsalted butter in the pan. Add the onions, carrots and leeks, and cook on medium heat until the onions appear clear.

Add the Arborio rice to the onion mixture and cook on medium to high heat for 2 minutes until the rice is translucent and well-coated with the oil and butter.

Heat the stock in a pot or microwave until just below boiling. Add the stock to the rice mixture one ladle at a time, stirring constantly until it is almost evaporated. Keep adding stock until the rice is tender and creamy but firm to the bite (about 25 to 30 minutes).

Add the mushrooms to the rice mixture and follow with the remaining butter, the Parmesan cheese and the flat leaf parsley. Stir mixture on medium heat for 2 minutes.

Peel prawn tails and cook in unsalted butter to which 1/4 cup (60 mL) of Vermouth has been added. Cook until opaque, but do not overcook. Remove the prawns and set aside.

Ladle rice into large Italian style dish and top with prawns. Decorate with a few sprigs of flat parsley and serve.

Michael Moscovich
Susie's on the Shore

Prawns and Vegetables in Coconut Sauce

Any vegetable in season can be used in this recipe. My favourite is green vegetables with a few fresh carrots.

	fresh prawns (or any white fish such as halibut)	
1 1/2 lbs	fresh vegetables, sliced in small pieces	1.25 kg
2 Tbsp	sesame oil	30 mL
1	onion, finely chopped	1
2	cloves garlic, crushed	2
1 tsp	sambal olek or 2 fresh chilies, seeded and chopped	5 mL
1 tsp	trasi (dried shrimp paste)	5 mL
2	strips lemon rind	2
1	large ripe tomato, peeled and chopped	1
2 cups	chicken stock	500 mL
1 1/2 cup	coconut milk	750 mL
3 tsp	peanut butter	15 mL
	salt, to taste	
1 Tbsp	lemon juice	15 mL

Precook fresh prawns and shell. Do not overcook. Set aside.

Heat oil in medium saucepan and fry onion until soft. Add garlic, sambal and trasi and fry over low heat for 2 minutes, crushing the trasi with the back of a spoon and stirring the mixture. Add lemon rind and tomato. Stir and cook to a pulp.

Add stock and bring to a simmering point with the lid off. Add the vegetables according to the time they take to cook. They should be tender but still crisp.

Add the coconut milk, peanut butter and stir to dissolve peanut butter. Add the cooked prawns (or cooked fish) and heat through, but do not bring to a boil (because coconut milk will curdle).

Set aside for a few minutes. Add lemon juice and stir. Serve with rice.

Georges Lalonde

Specially Spiced Prawns

24	large shrimp (or prawns) peeled and deveined	24

Seasoning

1 tsp	ground cayenne pepper	5 mL
1/2 tsp	black pepper	2 mL
1/2 tsp	salt	2 mL
1/2 tsp	dried thyme leaves, crushed	2 mL
1 tsp	dried basil leaves, crushed	5 mL
1/2 tsp	dried oregano leaves, crushed	2 mL
1/4 tsp	Worcestershire sauce	1 mL
1/3 cup	butter or margarine	75 mL
11/2 tsp	garlic, minced	7 mL
1/4 cup	beer, room temperature	60 mL
1	large tomato, coarsely diced	1

Clean and devein the shrimp under cold running water. Drain well and set aside.

In a small bowl combine the cayenne pepper, black pepper, salt, thyme, basil and oregano.

Combine the butter, garlic, Worcestershire sauce, and the seasonings from small bowl. Mix in a large skillet (wok) over high heat.

When the butter is melted, add the tomato, then the shrimp. Cook 2 minutes, stirring evenly.

Add the beer and cover and cook 1 minute longer.

Remove from heat.

Serve with rice, French bread and Caesar salad.

Sharon Arbour
Campbell River Lodge

Fried Jumbo Prawns
in Spicy Sweet and Sour Sauce

1 lb	jumbo prawns	500 g
1/2 tsp	salt	2 mL
1/2 tsp	white pepper	2 mL
3 Tbsp	cornstarch	45 mL
1 piece	green pepper	1 piece
1 piece	red pepper	1 piece
1 piece	fresh red chili pepper	1 piece
2 slices	pineapple	2 slices
1 tsp	chopped garlic	5 mL
1/2 tsp`	chopped ginger	2 mL

Sauce

2 1/2 Tbs	red wine	38 mL
3 Tbsp	Splenda sugar	45 mL
	(or any low calorie sweetener)	
1 1/2 Tbs	ketchup	38 mL
1/3 tsp	salt	1.5 mL
1/3 tsp	sesame oil	1.5 mL
1/3 cup	water	75 mL
1 1/2 tsp	cornstarch	7 mL
1 tsp	chili paste	5 mL

Peel prawns from shells. Marinate in salt, white pepper and cornstarch for half an hour. Cut green pepper, red pepper, chili pepper and pineapple into pieces.

Fry prawns in hot oil until golden brown. Take out and drain. Leave for later use.

Combine sauce ingredients.

Heat 1 tablespoon oil (15 mL) and sauté mashed garlic and chopped ginger. Add peppers and pineapple, stir well.
Add sautéed garlic, ginger, peppers and pineapple to sauce, stir well, and bring to a boil. Add in jumbo prawns, stir well. Dish up and serve.

Joseph Au
Best Wok

Barbequed Prawns

2 lbs	frozen prawns, large size	1 kg
1 cup	olive oil	250 mL
2 Tbsp	fresh lime juice	30 mL
1/4 cup	combination of fresh mint, parsley, oregano and thyme, chopped	60 mL
2 tsp	pressed garlic	10 mL

Thaw prawns (this takes 2 to 3 hours), then pat fairly dry.

Combine olive oil, lime juice, mint, parsley, oregano, thyme and garlic to make marinade.

Marinate prawns for 30 minutes at room temperature, stirring 2 to 3 times.

Place prawns on fish rack/grill on barbeque at high heat.

Stir while cooking to keep from burning. Cook 2 to 3 minutes until prawns have turned opaque.

Remove from heat and serve immediately, as prawns will continue to cook.

Don't overcook!

Serves 6

**Barb Shook
Photographer**

Shrimp Fra Diavolo with Linguine

Fra diavolo, with its abundance of hot red pepper and attendant fiery nature, may be named for the devil - its literal translation from the Italian is "brother devil" - but it can do an angel's work for home cooks. How so? Shrimp fra diavolo, a seriously garlicky, spicy, winey tomato sauce studded with shrimp and served over pasta, takes less than 30 minutes from start to finish.

1 lb	medium-large shrimp (preferably 31 to 35 count, peeled (and deveined, if desired)	500 g
1 tsp	crushed red pepper flakes (or more to taste)	,5 mL
6 Tbsp	extra-virgin olive oil	90 mL
1 1/2 Tbs	salt	23 mL
1/4 cup	cognac or brandy	60 mL
4 Tbsp	garlic, minced or pressed through garlic press (about 12 medium), 8 large, or 5 extra large cloves)	60 mL
1/2 tsp	sugar	2 mL
28 oz	can diced tomatoes, drained	796 mL
1 cup	medium-dry white wine, such as Sauvignon Blanc	250 mL
1/4 cup	minced fresh parsley leaves	60 mL
1 lb	linguine or spaghetti	500 g

Bring 4 quarts (4 L) water to rolling boil, covered, in large Dutch oven or stockpot.

While water is heating, heat 12 inch (30 cm) heavy-bottomed skillet over high heat for 4 minutes.

Meanwhile, toss shrimp, half of red pepper flakes, 2 tablespoons (30 mL) olive oil, and 3/4 teaspoon (4 mL) salt in medium bowl.

Add shrimp to skillet and quickly spread in single layer; cook, without stirring, until bottoms of shrimp turn spotty brown, about 30 seconds.

Off heat, stir to turn shrimp, and add cognac; let stand off heat until cognac warms slightly, about 5 seconds, and return pan to high heat. Wave lit match over skillet until cognac ignites; shake skillet until flames subside, transfer shrimp to medium bowl, and set aside.

Off heat, cool now-empty skillet 2 minutes, return to burner and reduce heat to low. Add 3 tablespoons (45 mL) olive oil and 3 tablespoons (45 mL) garlic; cook, stirring constantly, until garlic foams and is sticky and straw-coloured, 7 to 10 minutes.

Add remaining red pepper flakes, 3/4 teaspoon (4 mL) salt, sugar, tomatoes and wine; increase heat to medium-high, and simmer until thickened and fragrant, about 8 minutes.

Stir in reserved shrimp and accumulated juices, remaining 1 tablespoon (15 mL) garlic and parsley and simmer until shrimp have heated through, about 1 minute longer. Off heat, stir in remaining 1 tablespoon (15 mL) olive oil.

While sauce simmers, add linguine or spaghetti and remaining 1 tablespoon (15 mL) salt to boiling water, stir to separate pasta, cover, and cook until al dente; reserve 1/3 cup (75 mL) pasta cooking water and drain pasta.

Transfer drained pasta back to now-empty Dutch oven or stock-pot; add about 1/2 cup (125 mL) sauce (without shrimp) and 2 to 3 tablespoons (30 to 45 mL) reserved pasta cooking water; toss to coat.

Divide pasta among warm serving bowls, top with a portion of sauce and shrimp, and serve immediately.

Serves 4 to 6

Kathy Morrison
Something Special

Pad Phong Ka-ri

Use one kind of seafood only or any combination of the seafood that you desire.

	prawns, mussels, crab	
2 Tbsp	canola oil	30 mL
1 tsp	minced garlic	5 mL
1 Tbsp	fish sauce	15 mL
1 Tbsp	oyster sauce	15 mL
1 Tbsp	Maggi seasoning	15 mL
1 tsp	sugar	5 mL
1 tsp	curry powder	5 mL
	celery, mushrooms, broccoli, good-size chunks	
	green onion, sliced	
1/2 cup	cream	125 mL
	ground black pepper	

Heat oil and garlic in pan on high.

Add seafood, celery, mushrooms, broccoli and green onions. Cook on high for 2 minutes.

Add fish sauce, oyster sauce and Maggi. Cook on high for 1 minute.

Add cream. Sprinkle with ground black pepper and serve.

Auttawee Mongkolsute
Baan Thai Restaurant

Shrimp Chow Mein with Egg Noodles

This makes a complete meal. Just add some spring rolls and dipping sauce.

7 oz	peeled shrimp	200 g
1/2 lb	egg chow mein noodles	225 g
1	large onion, chopped	1
2 Tbsp	peanut oil	30 mL
1 tsp	Chinese five-spice powder	5 mL
1	large zucchini, cut into matchsticks	1
1	medium carrot, cut into matchsticks	1
1	green bell pepper, seeded and julienne	1
1	jalapeno pepper, seeded and minced	1
2	cloves of garlic, minced	2
2	large handfuls of bean sprouts	2
1/4 cup	sherry	60 mL
1/4 cup	soy sauce	60 mL
1/2 cup	water	125 mL

Soak the noodles in boiling water until soft.

Cook the onion in oil in a large pan or wok until soft but not browned. Stir in the five-spice powder and cook for 1 minute.

Add zucchini, carrots, green pepper, jalapeno pepper and garlic. Stir-fry for 3 to 4 minutes.

Drain noodles and add to pan.

Add the shrimp and bean sprouts.

Mix the sherry, soy sauce and water together and add to the pan.

Cook for 2 to 3 minutes, tossing together.

Serves 4

Quality Foods

Sundried Tomato Fettucini with Prawns and Scallops

Prawns and scallops
Fettucini

Sundried Tomato Sauce

1/2 cup	butter	125 mL
	garlic	
1 cup	sundried tomatoes, chopped	250 mL
4 cups	whipping cream	1 L
1 Tbsp	sugar	15 mL
1 Tbsp	Dijon mustard	15 mL
1 tsp	salt	5 mL

Melt butter, sauté garlic, add tomatoes. Simmer 2 minutes.

Add cream and Dijon mustard. Simmer 5 minutes.

Add sugar and salt to taste.

Sauté prawns and scallops until thoroughly cooked.

Add to sundried tomato sauce. Toss with your favourite cooked pasta.

Carol
Seadrift Fish Market
Nanaimo

Lemon-Garlic Shrimp

1 lb	shrimp, peeled and deveined	500 g
1/4 cup	butter	60 mL
2 Tbsp	olive oil	30 mL
2	green onions, diced	2
4	garlic cloves, minced	4
1/2 cup	white wine	125 mL
1/4 cup	chicken broth	60 mL
1 Tbsp	oregano flakes	15 mL
2	dashes Tabasco	2
1 tsp	anchovy paste (optional)	5 mL
1	lemon (juice only)	1
	a sprinkle of Parmesan cheese	
	chopped parsley	

Over medium heat, sauté green onions in butter and oil until soft.

Add garlic and sauté until almost golden.

Add white wine, chicken broth, oregano, Tabasco, anchovy paste and lemon juice. Increase heat and reduce mixture by half.

Add shrimp and cook until shrimp are pink.

Remove cooked shrimp to a warmed bowl.

Continue reducing mixture until it starts to thicken. Pour over shrimp; sprinkle with Parmesan cheese and chopped parsley.

Serve with crusty bread and a tossed salad.

Gordon LeMay

Baked Shrimp and Feta Cheese Sauce over Linguine

1 lb	medium shrimp	500 g
1 tsp	olive oil	5 mL
3/4 tsp	dried oregano	4mL
1/2 tsp	salt	2 ml
1/4 tsp	crushed red pepper	1 mL
3	cloves garlic, crushed	3
	cooking spray	
1/2 cup	white wine	125 mL
3 cups	diced plum tomatoes	750 mL
3/4 cup	crumbled Feta cheese	175 mL
4 cups	hot cooked linguine	1 L
1/4 cup	fresh basil, chopped	60 mL

Preheat oven to 350° F (180° C.)

Heat oil over medium heat and add shrimp and spices and sauté for 5 minutes.

Spoon shrimp mixture into a baking dish coated with cooking spray.

Return pan to heat and add wine to skillet and cook until reduced to approximately 1/4 cup (60 mL), about 3 minutes.

Stir in tomatoes and pour over shrimp. Sprinkle with cheese and bake for 10 minutes.

Meanwhile cook pasta and drain.

Pour sauce over pasta and sprinkle with fresh basil.

Serves 4

Quality Foods

Spaghettini in Crab Sauce

2 cups	crab meat	500 mL
1/4 cup	extra virgin olive oil	60 mL
2	garlic cloves, crushed	2
28 oz	can diced plum tomatoes, with juice	796 mL
	salt and pepper, to taste	
1/4 cup	parsley, finely chopped	60 mL
1 lb	spaghettini	450 g
	freshly ground Parmesan cheese, to taste	

In a large frypan over medium heat, heat the oil and add the garlic. Cook for 2 minutes, then add the tomatoes and salt and pepper.

Cook over medium-low heat for 20 minutes.

Meanwhile, cook the pasta until al dente.

Add the parsley and crab meat to the sauce and let simmer for 5 minutes.

Drain the pasta and add the pasta to the frypan and toss over high heat for 1 minute.

Divide among heated pasta bowls and sprinkle Parmesan over.

Serves 4

Quality Foods

Poached Oysters

12	fresh oysters, shucked, meat and liquor removed and saved, shells washed	12
1 Tbsp	shallots, minced	15 mL
2 Tbsp	butter	30 mL
	ground pepper	
1 cup	white wine	250 mL
1/2 cup	cream	125 mL
	beurre manie (1 Tbsp/15 mL butter and 1 Tbsp/15 mL flour kneaded together to form a paste)	
2 Tbsp	butter	30 mL
1 Tbsp	parsley, chopped	15 mL
	mushrooms, truffles and/or almonds, (optional)	

Warm the shells in the oven.

Put the oysters and their juice in a pan. Add minced shallots, butter, ground pepper and white wine.

Poach until the oysters plump. Don't overcook.

Remove the oysters and reduce the sauce by half.

When the sauce has reduced, add cream and bring to a boil. Add buerre manie, small pieces at a time, whisking it in until the sauce is of the desired thickness.

After you add beurre manie, you may add mushrooms, truffles and /or almonds to the sauce.

Add butter and chopped parsley.

Put the oysters in their shells and pour the sauce over them.

Serve immediately.

Serves 2

Originally from Willa Budge

Sesame Oysters

6	Talbot Cove oysters (sweet deepwater oysters from local waters)	6
1 cup	seasoned flour	250 mL
1/2 cup	toasted sesame seeds	125 mL
1 Tbsp	olive oil (Pommace)	15 mL

Sauce

1/2 cup	Balsamic vinegar	125 mL
1/4 cup	demerara sugar	60 mL
1/8 cup	fresh lemon juice	30 mL
1/2 tsp	finely minced ginger	2 mL
1/2 Tbsp	finely minced garlic	7 mL
1/4 cup	chili oil	60 mL
1 Tbsp	Worcestershire sauce	15 mL
1/2 cup	soy sauce (Kikkoman)	125 mL

Mix and stir the sauce ingredients.
Note: Sauce recipe is for 2 batches of oysters. It improves as it sits in the fridge!

Preheat non-stick or seasoned frying pan. Add olive oil.

Dredge oysters in seasoned flour, then add to hot oil, frying 1 minute on one side only.

With tongs, remove oysters and dip the cooked side into toasted sesame seeds, then return to pan raw side down and finish cooking, 1 or 2 minutes.

Add sauce (half the recipe) until it bubbles.

Serve immediately over rice or oriental noodle dish.
Bon Appetite!

Chef Ralf Spodzieja
Painter's Lodge

Pan-Fried Oysters

A variation from the traditional pan-fried oysters that are dipped in egg wash, coated with cracker crumbs and fried in cooking oil.

1-2 pints	oysters, rinsed and drained *	500 mL - 1 L
2	eggs	2
1/2 cup	milk	125 mL
	salt and pepper, to taste	
1 tsp	garlic powder	5 mL
1 cup	biscuit mix	250 mL
1 cup	Italian breadcrumbs	250 mL
1 cup	flour	250 mL

Beat together eggs, milk, salt, pepper and garlic powder.

Mix together biscuit mix, breadcrumbs and flour.

Dip oysters in egg wash and coat with breading mix.

Fry in 1/2 inch (1.25 cm) cooking oil in fry pan for 3 or 4 minutes over medium heat until oysters are golden brown on both sides.

Garnish and serve.

*If a firmer oyster is preferred, blanch oysters in boiling water for 2 to 3 minutes before dipping in egg wash.

Xinh Dwelley
Taylor Shellfish Farms

Harbour Grill Baked Oysters

1 pint	Fanny Bay oysters	500 mL
1/2 cup	butter	125 mL
1 1/2 cup	breadcrumbs	375 mL
	salt and pepper	
1/2 tsp	cumin	2 mL
1/2 cup	heavy cream	125 mL
1 tsp	Worcestershire sauce	5 mL

Cut oysters into bite-size pieces. Save the liquid.

Mix butter, breadcrumbs, salt, pepper and cumin.

Layer half the breadcrumbs in a casserole dish. Add oysters.

Mix Worcestershire sauce, cream and oyster liquid. Pour over oysters. Cover with remaining the breadcrumbs.

Bake at 350° F (180 ° C) for 40 minutes.

Mike Zbinden
Harbour Grill

Oysters Rockefeller a la Suz

All too often, recipes for the traditional Oysters Rockefeller are way too complicated to make; too many steps to follow. Thus Suz's simplified version.

24	oysters	24
Sauce		
1/2 or 1	small onion, chopped	1/2 or 1
2	cloves garlic, chopped	2
	butter or oil to sauté	
1	large spinach or the equivalent	1
	young shoots of stinging nettle	
	oyster liquor	
1-2 Tbsp	Pernod	15 - 30 mL
	crushed red pepper	
	grated cheese (Gruyere, Cheddar	
	or even Parmesan)	

Oysters
Rinse oysters to remove sand and grit. Shuck oysters, reserving liquor if possible. Remove any broken shell from each oyster.

Place oysters in their shells (cupside) and lay on baking sheet that will fit a broiler oven. Rock salt or crumpled tinfoil can be used to stabilize the oysters. Now you are ready for the sauce.

Sauce
Sauté chopped onion and garlic in butter or oil until lightly browned. Add spinach or stinging nettles and cook until barely wilted.

Place mixture in blender or food processor adding enough cream or oyster liquor to process the vegetables. A very thick but not too finely puréed sauce is what you are aiming for. Add the Pernod and red pepper, if desired.

Putting them together
Spoon some sauce on each oyster and top with grated cheese. Place in broiler until cheese is browned. Remove and enjoy alone or with some friends, if you can bear to share!

Brent Petkau
Oysterman

Red Curried Mussels

1 1/2 lbs	mussels	750 g
2/3 cup	fish stock or water	150 mL
1 Tbsp	rice wine vinegar	15 mL
2 Tbsp	kaffir lime leaves, chopped	30 mL
2	cloves garlic	2
2 Tbsp	vegetable oil	30 mL
1	onion, chopped	1
3 Tbsp	red curry paste	45 mL
1 1/2 cup	coconut cream	375 mL

Scrub mussels with a hard brush, and using a small sharp knife, pull out and discard the beards. Discard mussels that will not stay closed.

Bring fish stock, rice wine vinegar and 1 garlic clove to the boil. Add mussels and simmer, covered until they open, about 5 minutes. Discard mussels that do not open.

Remove mussels, pull off and discard top shells and keep warm. Strain cooking liquid and reserve.

Heat oil and sauté onion, remaining garlic clove and kaffir lime leaves until soft.

Add red curry paste, stirring for 1 minute.

Add reserved liquid and coconut cream. Bring to the boil, reduce heat and simmer for 3 minutes.

Add mussels and serve hot with rice. (Red Thai rice, black rice or Jasmine rice).

Amy Concepcion
Amy's Asian Foods & Cafe

Steamed Thai Mussels

Calculate 1 pound (500 g) of mussels per person. Preferably use the BC Honey Mussel. Make sure the mussels are debearded and clean. Do not use open mussels. Other mussels could be used from Salt Spring Island or the PEI mussel, which is slightly smaller with less meat.

6 lbs	mussels	2.75 kg
6	medium coloured peppers (red, yellow and green), seeded and thinly sliced	6
2	large red onions, sliced	2
2	carrots, peeled and thinly cut matchsticks (batonnetes)	2
2 - 3	pieces Galangal, soaked (available in an Asian Grocery Store)	2 - 3
2 - 3	lime leaves (Asian Grocery Store)	2 - 3
1	small package yellow Thai curry paste	1
3	14 oz (398 mL) cans coconut milk	3
3	cloves garlic, minced	3
1	bunch of chopped cilantro	1
8	green onions, cut Oriental style	8
1	bunch of whole cilantro, for garnish	1
1 lb	bean sprouts	500 mL
2 oz	fish base	60 mL
3 oz	peanut or canola oil	90 mL

Use a large stock or soup pot to cook this dish. You can also cook this recipe in two batches if you don't have a large enough pot.

Sauté peppers and onions. Add lime leaves, galagal and garlic.

Pour in coconut milk and add 1/3 of the Thai curry paste. If you like a spicier sauce, add more curry paste to it.

Add the fish base and the matchstick carrots and bring to a boil.

Add cleaned and debearded mussels into pot and cover with lid. Cook for about 5 minutes. Make sure you shake the pot often to turn and cook the mussels evenly.

Once the mussels have opened up, check for taste and add the chopped cilantro and the green onions.

You can serve this dish with steamed rice. Ladle the juice on top of the mussels.

Use bean sprouts and cilantro as garnish.

Enjoy!

Serves 6

Executive Chef Hansi Zihlmann
The Brasserie Restaurant
Coast Discovery Inn and Marina

Linguine with Mussels

Serve with a fresh baguette and a fresh salad.

24	mussels, scrubbed and debearded	24
1 Tbsp	olive oil	15 mL
1/4 cup	shallots, minced	60 mL
2 Tbsp	garlic, minced	30 mL
2 cups	white wine	500 mL
1/2 cup	chicken stock	125 mL
3 Tbsp	fresh parsley, chopped	45 mL
	salt and pepper, to taste	
1/2 lb	linguine - cooked and tossed with olive oil	225 g
1/2 cup	Parmesan cheese, freshly grated	125 mL
1 Tbsp	parsley	15 mL

In a large frying pan, heat the olive oil. When the oil is hot, add the shallots and garlic and sauté for 4 minutes.

Add the wine and chicken stock.

Bring to a boil, add the mussels, cover and reduce heat to a simmer. Cook for 3 to 4 minutes or until the shells open.

Stir in the parsley and season with salt and pepper.

Add the cooked pasta and heat through.

Divide the pasta between two bowls and spoon mussels over. Garnish with the grated Parmesan and parsley.

Serves 2

Quality Foods

Mediterranean Mussels in Curry Sauce

5 lb	mussels	2.25 kg
3 cups	water	750 mL
1/4 cup	butter or olive oil	60 mL
1 tsp	garlic, finely chopped	5 mL
3/4 cup	onion, coarsely chopped	175 mL
8 oz	canned coconut milk	250 mL
1 Tbsp	curry powder	15 mL
1 1/2 Tbs	soy sauce	23 mL
	salt and pepper, to taste	
1/2 tsp	sugar or honey	2 mL
1/2 cup	ground peanuts (dry roasted and unsalted)	125 mL
	cayenne pepper (optional)	
	green onion, chopped (for garnish)	
	cilantro, chopped (for garnish)	

Steam mussels until open. Drain and remove meats from shells; set meats aside.

In a frying pan, lightly brown garlic in butter. Add onion and sauté until clear.

To the onion and garlic mixture, add coconut milk, curry powder, soy sauce, salt, pepper, sugar, peanuts and cayenne pepper; mixing well in the order given. Add mussels last.

Bring back to a boil to warm up mussels.

Add chopped green onion and chopped cilantro just before serving for a final garnish.

Serve over rice or noodles. Enjoy.

Serves 2 people or 4 light eaters

Xinh Dwelley
Taylor Shellfish Farms

Hard Cider and Pears with Mussels

The key is to make sure that your mussels are very fresh. Don't be afraid to ask the fishmonger to let you open a mussel and see that the body of the mussel fills the shell up to the pale blue silver spoon that the mussels rest in. If you can see a difference in colour just above the top of the mussel, it's not fresh and will shrink when cooked.

4 lbs	fresh mussels	2 kg
12 oz	can of clam nectar	341 mL
12 oz	bottle of good Hard Pear or Apple Cider	341 mL
4	large firm ripe pears	4
2	large French onions (the purple skinned onions) green curry paste, to taste (found in the gourmet section of your grocery store)	2

Peel the pears and cut into quarters.

Peel the French onions and cut into quarters.

Place in a roasting pan, bake at 350° F (180° C) until the pears and onions are translucent and very soft; do not brown. This will take about 30 minutes.

While the pears and onions are baking, wash the mussels in cold water, removing any sea life. Pull the beard from the mussel by pulling from the top of the mussel down to the hinge. Rinse again.

When the pears and onions are soft, add the clam nectar and the Hard Cider and purée in a food processor or hand held food puréer, until smooth. The mixture will look like a creamy broth. This will be hot, so be sure to be cautious if you are transferring the ingredients to a food processor. If you use a food processor, return the creamy mixture to the pan.

Add the green curry paste, a little at a time, to the creamy mixture. Start with a teaspoon (5 mL) at a time. This dish is delicate, be sure not to over do the curry, you are only after a hint of the green curry; it should be a background flavour, and should not overpower the delicate mussels.

With the creamy mixture in the roasting pan, place on the stove top and bring to a rolling simmer. Place the mussels in the pan, put the lid on and steam for about 5 minutes. Do not overcook. Peek in and make sure the mussels are open.

Serve the mussels in large soup bowls, ladle the Pear Hard Cider broth over the mussels and serve immediately.

This dish can be served as an appetizer or a main course. The secret is to not overcook the mussels, and to make sure they are very fresh. Do not buy mussels that are open, or even slightly open; be picky.

Serves 4

If you make this for a bigger group simply continue to double the recipe.

Silky Pearce
Silky's Bed and Breakfast

Clams in Black Bean Sauce

4 - 5 lbs	Manilla or Littleneck clams	2 kg
1/4 cup	butter or margarine	60 mL
1	medium onion, sliced	1
1 Tbsp	chopped lemongrass	15 mL
1	clove minced garlic	1
3 Tbsp	cooking sherry	45 mL
1/2 tsp	salt (optional)	2 mL
3/4 tsp	black pepper	4 mL
2 Tbsp	sesame seed oil	30 mL
3 Tbsp	black bean (Hoisin), do not drain	45 mL
1	green onion, chopped (for garnish)	1

Melt butter and brown garlic.

In a pan with a fitted lid, large enough to hold 5 pounds (2 kg) of clams, add onion, lemongrass, garlic, sherry, salt, pepper and sesame oil.

Sauté lightly, add 3/4 cup (175 mL) of water and bring to a boil.

Add washed clams to mixture. Mix well and cover.

Bring to a boil until clams open.

Sprinkle green onions on top and cover for 5 minutes.

Serve and enjoy.

Taylor Shellfish Farms

Spicy Clam Linguine

2 Tbsp	olive oil	30 mL
1	small onion, diced	1
1	clove garlic, minced	1
1 Tbsp	chili peppers, crushed	15 mL
1	can baby clams	1
	or	
2 lbs	whole clams	1 kg
1 cup	white wine	250 mL
1 lb	cooked linguine	500 g

Garnish

red and green peppers, diced
tomatoes, diced
green onions, chopped
Parmesan cheese

Sauté onions and garlic in hot olive oil until soft. Add clams, chilies and wine. (If using whole clams, cover and steam until shells open).

While that is cooking, have linguine heating in hot water bath.

When ingredients are hot, drain pasta, place everything into large bowl and toss together.

Served topped with your choice of garnishes.

Serves 4

Sheila Bennett
The Willows Neighbourhood Pub

Seafood Fettucini

3.5 oz	fresh shrimp, prawns or scallops	100 g
2 Tbsp	butter	30 mL
1/2 cup	Parmesan cheese	125 mL
1/2 cup	dry white wine	125 mL
1/2	of each, medium-size yellow, green and red peppers, sliced in very thin strips	1/2
1	carrot, sliced in very thin long sticks to match the pepper strips	1
2	pieces celery, sliced in very thin long sticks	2
1/2 cup	mushrooms, chopped	125 mL
1/2 cup	onions, finely chopped	125 mL
1	small head of broccoli, sliced in strips	1
1/2 cup	cup fresh parsley, finely chopped	125 mL
2	cloves garlic, crushed or chopped very fine	2
	fresh ground pepper to taste - use seasoned pepper for added colour	
	salt to taste	
2 cups	whipping cream	500 mL
	fettucini	
dash	paprika	dash

While the water is heating for the fettucini, begin making the sauce.

In a large skillet, melt the butter over medium heat. When the butter has melted, sauté garlic and seafood very lightly for a minute. Do not overcook.

Add freshly ground black pepper or seasoned pepper. Add white wine and allow to simmer until white wine bubbles slightly.

Add whipping cream all at once, stirring constantly. Make sure that the temperature is not too high when adding the whipping cream or you will have cottage cheese.

Bring the sauce up to temperature. When the sauce begins to steam and thicken, ever so slightly, begin adding the Parmesan cheese, 1 tablespoon (15 mL) at a time, stirring constantly. When all the cheese has been added, allow it to simmer until the sauce has thickened slightly.

While the sauce is thickening, lightly sauté the vegetables in butter for a few moments.

Add cooked and drained fettucini to the sauce skillet and mix thoroughly to coat the pasta. The sauce should still be fairly thin as the pasta will absorb a lot of the liquid.

Then add the vegetables and parsley and mix thoroughly. If the sauce is still very thin, allow to cook a couple of minutes longer, otherwise serve immediately.

Serve all plates at one time so that everything is divided up equally. Pour the extra sauce over each plate, sprinkle with a bit of grated Parmesan and a dash of paprika and serve.

You can also add any other type of seafood as long as you cut it so that it is all the same size as the shrimp.

It is important that the sauce and the pasta be finished at the same time. Don't overcook the pasta.

Bertha Seabolt

Asparagus and Scallop Stir-Fry

This is a quick and easy stir-fry that everyone will love!

3/4 lb	scallops, cut in half	375 g
1 lb	asparagus, cut diagonally	500 g
3/4 cup	chicken broth	175 mL
1 Tbsp	cornstarch	15 mL
1 tsp	light soy sauce	5 mL
1 tsp	sesame oil	5 mL
1 cup	mushrooms, sliced	250 mL
2	garlic cloves, minced	2
1 cup	cherry tomatoes, cut in half	250 mL
3	green onions, sliced diagonally at 1/2 inch (1.25 cm)	3

Cook asparagus in boiling water until tender-crisp.

Combine chicken broth, cornstarch, soy sauce and sesame oil and set aside.

Stir-fry garlic, scallops and mushrooms in a little olive oil until cooked through (about 4 minutes).

Add cornstarch mixture and cook until thickened.

Add asparagus, tomatoes and green onion. Heat through.

Add pepper to taste and serve over rice.

Serves 4

Quality Foods

Grilled Scallops

24	large scallops - approximately 1 1/2 lbs (750 g)	24
	salt and pepper, to taste	
1 Tbsp	olive oil	15 mL
1	clove garlic, minced	1
3 Tbsp	fresh ginger, grated	45 mL
4 Tbsp	soy sauce	60 mL
4 Tbsp	dry Sherry or Vermouth	60 mL
	juice of 1 lemon	
4	green onions, finely minced	4
24	small cherry tomatoes	24
6	skewers	6

Place the scallops in a glass dish. Sprinkle with salt and pepper.

Whisk together the oil, garlic, ginger, soy sauce, sherry, lemon juice and green onion.

Pour over the scallops and marinade for 1 hour.

Drain the scallops, reserving the marinade.

Place 4 scallops on each skewer alternating with a cherry tomato.

Grill for 5 minutes per side, brushing with the marinade after turning.

Serve with rice pilaf and sautéed medley of vegetables.

Makes 6 skewers

Chef Dwight Walden
North Island College
Cook Training Program

Saffron and Star Anise Seafood Bowl with Moroccan Couscous and Grilled Eggplant

16	fresh blue mussels	16
16	fresh Manilla clams	16
6	large Westcoast prawns	6
4	medium scallops	4
1 Tbsp	ground star anise	15 mL
pinch	saffron	pinch
pinch	sea salt	pinch
pinch	fresh cracked black pepper	pinch
1 Tbsp	garlic, minced	15 mL
1 Tbsp	shallots, minced	15 mL
1 Tbsp	honey	15 mL
1 cup	canned crushed tomatoes	250 mL
1/2 cup	Chardonay (white wine)	125 mL
1 cup	fish stock	250 mL
1/2 cup	Spanish onion, julienne	125 mL
1/2 cup	leeks, julienne	125 mL
1/2 cup	red bell pepper, julienne	125 mL

In a 10 inch (22.5 cm) saucepan sauté garlic, shallots and spices. Add liquid and simmer for 3 minutes.

Add seafood and vegetables. Cover and simmer until shellfish have completely opened - 5 to 7 minutes.

Couscous

2 cup	couscous	500 mL
2 cups	chicken stock	500 mL
1 1/2 tsp	cumin seed, toasted and ground	7 mL
1 tsp	coriander seed, toasted and ground	5 mL
1/4 tsp	cinnamon	1 mL
1 tsp	garam marsala	5 mL
1/4 cup	cilantro, chopped	60 mL
1/2 cup	white onion, diced	125 mL
2 Tbsp	olive oil	30 mL

In a small saucepan, sauté onion until brown. Add cumin seed, coriander seed, cinnamon and garam marsala and cook for 2 minutes.

Add chicken stock to the pot and bring to a boil. Add couscous and reduce temperature, stirring constantly.

Remove from heat and cover. Let sit for 5 minutes. Stir in the cilantro.

Grilled Eggplant

1	**Japanese eggplant, sliced into**	**1**
	1 inch (2.5 cm) thick wedges	
3 Tbsp	**olive oil**	**45 mL**
1 Tbsp	**sesame oil**	**15 mL**
1 Tbsp	**white rice vinegar**	**15 mL**
1 tsp	**fenugreek seed, ground**	**5 mL**
1 tsp	**garam marsala**	**5 mL**
1/2 tsp	**brown mustard seed**	**2 mL**
1 Tbsp	**minced ginger**	**15 mL**
1 Tbsp	**minced garlic**	**15 mL**

In a large bowl, mix olive oil, sesame oil, white rice vinegar, fenugreek seed, garam marsala, brown mustard seed, ginger and garlic together. Add eggplant and toss until evenly coated.

Grill on hot grill for approximately 4 minutes each side.

Put couscous in center of bowl, arrange seafood around and your eggplant spears from rim.

Serves 2

Chef Ross Baker
Blue Water Bistro

Seared Scallops with Orzo Risotto

Serve with some steamed asparagus, a salad and a fresh baguette.

16	large scallops (large shrimp can be substituted)	16
2 Tbsp	olive oil	30 mL
	salt and pepper, to taste	
	freshly grated Parmesan cheese	

Orzo Risotto

1 2/3 cup	orzo	400 mL
1 Tbsp	olive oil	15 mL
1 cup	mushrooms, diced	250 mL
1/3 cup	onions, diced	75 mL
1/3 cup	sundried tomatoes, diced	75 mL
1/3 cup	red pepper, diced	75 mL
2 cups	chicken stock	500 mL
1/2 cup	freshly grated Parmesan cheese	125 mL
2 Tbsp	chopped parsley	30 mL
1/2 cup	whipping cream	125 mL

Cook orzo according to package directions and set aside.

In a large pot, heat oil and sauté mushrooms, onion, sundried tomatoes and red pepper until soft. Add stock and bring to a boil. Stir in orzo, Parmesan and parsley.

Add cream and simmer gently, stirring frequently, until mixture is creamy but not runny - about 20 minutes.

Meanwhile, heat oil in a very hot pan. Season scallops with salt and pepper and sear until brown on the outside and opaque in the center.

Sprinkle Parmesan over risotto and top with scallops.

Serves 4

Quality Foods

Pan-Fried Seafood with Fruit

8 oz	prawns	250 g
2 oz	scallops	60 g
1	apple	1
1	stick celery	1
2	slices pineapple	2
1 tsp	garlic, chopped	5 mL
3 cups	oil	750 mL

Seasonings

1/2 tsp	salt	2 mL
1 tsp	lemon juice	5 mL
1/4 tsp	salt	1 mL
1	egg white	1
1 tsp	corn flour	5 mL
1/2 tsp	Shao-hsing wine	2 mL
1/5 tsp	salt	1 mL
1/3 tsp	corn flour	1.5 mL

Cut the celery into 1 1/2 inch (4 cm) portions. Cut the head and bottom off the apple and decore it. Dice it into small pieces. Marinate in seasoning for 10 minutes.

Wash the prawns and scallops and dry them thoroughly. Marinate in seasoning for 30 minutes.

Heat 3 cups oil in a wok on medium heat. Gently put in the shrimp, scallops, celery and then the diced apple. Fry until the prawns change colour, then drain the excess oil.

Leave 1 teaspoon (5 mL) oil in the wok. Quick fry the chopped garlic, then mix the prawns, scallops, celery, pineapple, apple and seasoning together. Finally add corn flour water to thicken.

Enjoy!

Sam Leung
Chan's Kitchen

Lobster Gordon'Burg

4	1 1/2 lb (675 g) fresh boiled lobsters	4
1	egg yolk	1
2 cups	heavy cream	500 mL
2 Tbsp	butter	30 mL
2	shallots, finely diced	2
1/2 lb	fresh mushrooms, cleaned and sliced	250 g
1/4 cup	Madeira wine or dry Sambuca	50 mL
1 tsp	chopped parsley	5 mL
	salt and pepper	
	dash of cayenne	

Boil lobster in a generous amount of water. Cover pan and simmer for 14 to 18 minutes. Water should boil not too rapidly. Shell will change to red colour.

Remove all meat from shell and dice. Set aside. Reserve shell for garnishing.

Mix egg yolk and 2 tablespoons (30 mL) of cream and set aside.

Heat butter in large skillet. When hot, add shallots and mushrooms and season well. Cook 3 minutes over medium-high heat.

Pour in wine or Sambuca. Cook 3 minutes on high heat.

Mix remaining cream, parsley and cayenne. Correct seasoning. Cook 4 to 5 minutes.

Add lobster meat and mix quickly.

Reduce to low and stir in egg yolk. Mix and cook for 2 minutes until thickened.

Serve on spinach pasta or your favourite pasta.

Gordo Walsh
Gordo's Uptown Cafe

Desserts

Dessert Coquille St. Jacques

There are four separate components to this dessert, but the end results are worth it! I created this dessert for one of our wine dinners in 2002. The theme of the dinner was B.C. Seafood and Wines. I thought that this would be the perfect ending to a seafood dinner. It had the right balance of attractiveness, pretension and taste and wit. Honestly, how often do you come across a seafood dessert?

Part 1

Scallop Shaped Chocolate Truffles

1 lb	Calbaut white chocolate (only), chopped	500 g
1 cup	heavy cream	250 mL

Boil the cream then add the chocolate to it. Stir until it looks homogenous. Then, let it cool in the refrigerator until it is the consistency of soft butter. Now it can be shaped into a ballotine, (a cylinder shaped roll), with a diameter of 1.5 inches (4 cm), using plastic wrap. Let it cool. Now it must be cut into slabs 3/4 inch (2 cm) thick and dipped into more melted Calbaut white chocolate.

1 lb	Calbaut white chocolate	500 g

This ingredient must be handled with care. In order to achieve melting and cooling perfection, it needs to be "tempered"; however that is a slightly advanced skill, so please ignore it. Instead, you must cut the chocolate before melting, into small pieces to aid in speedier melting. This will prevent the risk of exposing the chocolate to too much heat. The heat of the chocolate should be roughly the same as your lip.

Now that your chocolate is melted, you can dip the scallop shaped ganache into the melted white chocolate. Once it is covered, it should be placed onto some kitchen parchment and be allowed to cool in your fridge until needed.

Part 2

Scallop Shaped Tuille

1/2 lb	butter, room temperature	255 g
1 1/3 cup	icing sugar	310 g
1 cup	egg whites	255 g
1 1/3 cup	all purpose flour	310 g
2 - 10	large scallop shells	2 - 10
	(they can be purchased at a kitchen shop) You will need them for tracing to make a stencil and you will need them for shaping your cookies	
1	plastic shaped scallop shell stencil, which you must make out of a 4L ice cream bucket lid	1

For the tuille, the butter and icing sugar will have to be creamed in a food processor **"Not whipped"**. Then add, alternating the egg whites and the flour, until the cookie dough is smooth and homogenous.

Now the tuille batter can be scraped onto some parchment using the stencil and a palate knife.

The cookies should be baked at 400° F (200° C) oven for 4 minutes then quickly transferred onto greased-floured scallop shells.

The shells with the cookie now get baked for an additional 5 minutes.

Once they are cool, they must be stored in a sealable container, so they do not become stale, due to humidity.

Part 3

Cheese Sauce

1 lb	tub of Mascarpone cheese	500 g
	some liqueur of your choice for flavouring the cheese	

Easy method here, all you do is mix the cheese with the alcohol until a consistency of pudding is reached.

Part 4

Garnishes
1	cantaloupe	1
1	honeydew	1
	(These will be balled using a 5 mm parisienne scoop to simulate the effect of caviar)	
	strawberry	
	mint	
	strawberry coulis	
	crème anglaise	

I am not going to explain the assembly of this dessert because of the difficulty. Instead I have included a picture for your viewing pleasure.

"Good Luck"

Chef Trevor Forget
Gourmet by the Sea Restaurant

Index

April Point Seafood Hotpot, 59
Asian Delight, 22
Asparagus and Scallop Stir-Fry, 112
Baked Shrimp and Feta Cheese Sauce over Linguine, 94
Baked Oysters with Tomato, Parsley and Asiago Cheese, 28
Barbequed Oysters with Devil's Butter, 21
Barbequed Prawns, 87
Bouillabaisse, 62
Broiled Mussels on the Half Shell, 39
Cacciucco or Fish Stew, 56
Calgary Oysters, 32
California Roll, 76
Ceviche, 50
Chiopino, Seafood, 58
Chipotle and Cream Mussels, 40
Cioppino or Bouillabaisse, 62
Clams
    Clam Chowder, 64
    Clam Miso Soup, 65
    Clams in Black Bean Sauce, 108
    Sambuca Clams, 47
    Spicy Clam Linguine, 109
    Steamed Mussels or Clams, 46
Cortes Island Barbequed Oyster Variations, 22
Couscous, 114
Crab
    Crab Cakes with Pineapple Papaya Salsa, 74
    Crab Soup, 66
    Crabby Bob's Famous and Favourite Crab Dip, 16
    Extreme King Crab, 17
    Hot Crab Dip, 18
    Spaghettini in Crab Sauce, 95
    Stuffed Crab Claws, 19
    Sushi - California Roll, 76
Dessert Couquille St. Jacques, 120
Dorchester Hotel Shellfish, 45
Duke's Oyster Appy, 24
Extreme King Crab, 17
Fish Bait, 49
Fish Stew (Cacciucco), 56

Fresh Salsa Spritz, 51
Fried Jumbo Prawns in Spicy Sweet and Sour Sauce, 86
Glazed Oysters, 20
Grilled Eggplant, 115
Grilled Oyster Burger, 73
Grilled Prawn Caesar Salad, 68
Grilled Scallops, 113
Harbour Grill Baked Oysters, 99
Hard Cider and Pears with Mussels, 106
Hotpot
    April Point, 59
    Seafood, 60
Incredible Edibles from the Sea, 27
Lemon-Garlic Shrimp, 93
Linguine with Mussels, 104
Lobster Gordon'Burg, 118
Mediterranean Mussels in Curry Sauce, 105
Moules Munier, 37
Mussels
    Broiled Mussels on the Half Shell, 39
    Chipotle and Cream Mussels, 40
    Hard Cider and Pears with Mussels, 186
    Linguine with Mussels, 104
    Mediterranean Mussels in Curry Sauce, 105
    Moules Munier, 37
    Mussel Delight, 38
    Red Curried Mussels, 101
    Steamed Mussels or Clams, 46
    Steamed Thai Mussels, 102
    Swimming Scallops or Mussels, 44
    Tom's Mussels, 36
    West Coast Mussels, 41
    Wild Honey Mussels Sicilian Style, 35
Oysters
    Baked Oysters with Tomato, Parsley and Asiago Cheese, 28
    Barbequed Oysters with Devil's Butter, 21
    Calgary Oysters, 32
    Cortes Island Barbequed Oyster Variations, 22
    Duke's Oyster Appy, 24
    Glazed Oysters, 20
    Grilled Oyster Burger, 73
    Harbour Grill Baked Oysters, 99

Incredible Edibles from the Sea, 27
Ostras Gratinadas, 23
Oyster Misota, 26
Oyster Stew, 54
Oyster Stuffing for Turkey, 78
Oysters in Pernod Sauce, 29
Oysters with Champagne Sauce and Leeks, 30
Oysters with Mustard, 23
Oysters Rockefeller a la Suz, 100
Pan-Fried Oysters, 98
Poached Oysters, 96
Riptide Chef's Favourite Oysters, 33
Sambuca Oysters, 34
Sesame Oysters, 97
"Spiked" Oysters, 25
Sundance Oyster Wrap, 71
Pad Phong Ka-ri, 90
Pan-Fried Seafood with Fruit, 117
Pan Fried Oysters, 98
Pasta
Baked Shrimp and Feta Cheese Sauce over Linguine, 94
Linguine with Mussels, 104
Seafood Fettucini, 110
Shrimp Fra Diabolo with Linguine, 88
Spaghettini in Crab Sauce, 95
Spicy Clam Linguine, 109
Sundried Tomato Fettucini with Prawns and Scallops, 92
Poached Oysters, 96
Prawns
Barbequed Prawns, 87
Ceviche, 50
Fried Jumbo Prawns in Spicy Sweet and Sour Sauce, 86
Grilled Prawn Caesar Salad, 68
Pad Phong Ka-ri, 90
Prawns and Vegetables in Coconut Sauce, 84
Prawns with Cashew Nuts, 81
Specially Spiced Prawns, 85
Spicy Prawn Sauté with Basmati Rice Pilaf, 80
Sundried Tomato Fettucini with Prawns and Scallops, 92
West Coast Fish and Prawn Stew, 55
Wild Mushroom Risotto with Prawns, 82
Ragout, Seafood, 63
Red Curried Mussels, 101

Riptide Chef's Favourite Oysters, 33
Roast Pepper Tomato Sauce with Saffron and Pernod, 61
Saffron and Star Anise Seafood Bowl with
    Moroccan Couscous and Grilled Eggplant, 114
Salads
    Grilled Prawn Salad, 68
    West Coast Seafood Salad, 69
Salsas
    Pineapple Papaya Salsa, 75
    Fresh Salsa Spritz, 51
Sambuca Clams, 47
Sambuca Oysters, 34
Scallops
    Asparagus and Scallop Stir-Fry, 112
    Ceviche, 50
    Grilled Scallops, 113
    Scallops and Shrimp in White Wine, 42
    Scallops in Saffron Cream Sauce, 43
    Seared Scallops with Orzo Risotto, 116
    Shrimp and Scallop Gumbo, 67
    Sundried Tomato Fettucini with Prawns and Scallops, 92
Seafood
    April Point Seafood Hotpot, 59
    Bouillabaisse, 62
    Cacciucco (Fish Stew), 56
    Fish Bait, 49
    Pad Phong Ka-ri, 90
    Pan-Fried Seafood with Fruit, 117
    Saffron and Star Anise Seafood Bowl with
        Moroccan Couscous and Grilled Eggplant, 114
    Seafood Chiopino, 58
    Seafood Fettucini, 110
    Seafood Hotpot, 60
    Seafood Ragout, 63
    Spanakapita Wrap, 70
    West Coast Fish and Prawn Stew, 55
    West Coast Seafood Salad, 69
Seared Scallops with Orzo Risotto, 116
Sesame Oysters, 97
Shellfish
    Dorchester Hotel, 45

Shrimp
    Baked Shrimp and Feta Cheese Sauce over Linguine, 94
    Lemon-Garlic Shrimp, 93
    Scallops and Shrimp in White Wine, 42
    Shrimp and Avocado Wrap, 72
    Shrimp and Scallop Gumbo, 67
    Shrimp Chow Mein with Egg Noodles, 91
    Shrimp Fra Diavolo with Linguine, 88
    Shrimp Mousse, 48
    Shrimp Roll, 76
    Surprise Spread, 52
Smoked Oysters
    Incredible Edibles from the Sea, 27
Soups
    Clam Miso Soup, 65
    Crab Soup, 66
Spanakopita Wrap, 70
Spaghettini in Crab Sauce, 95
Specially Spiced Prawns, 85
Spicy Clam Linguine, 109
Spicy Prawn Sauté with Basmati Rice Pilaf, 80
"Spiked" Oysters, 25
Spinach and Feta Cheese Stuffing, 22
Steamed Mussels or Clams, 46
Steamed Thai Mussels, 102
Stir-Fry
    Asparagus and Scallop Stir-Fry, 112
 Stuffed Crab Claws, 19
Sundance Oyster Wrap, 71
Sundried Tomato Fettucini with Prawns and Scallops, 92
Surprise Spread, 52
Sushi Made Easy, 76
Swimming Scallops or Mussels, 44
Tom's Mussels, 36
West Coast Fish and Prawn Stew, 55
West Coast Seafood Salad, 69
Wild Honey Mussels Sicilian Style, 35
Wild Mushroom Risotto with Prawns, 82
Wraps
    Shrimp and Avocado Wrap, 72
    Spanakopita Wrap, 70
    Sundance Oyster Wrap, 71

Also Available in this Series:

Salmon
C O O K E R Y
From the Salmon Capital of the World

Chefs, restaurants and the salmon industry of Campbell River, the "Salmon Capital of the World", have contributed their very best recipes in this salmon only cookbook.

The first in the series produced as a fundraiser for the Canadian Diabetes Association, Team Diabetes Canada.

For ordering information:
email: info@kaskgraphics.com